A PATHWAY TO PROFIT

CULTURE IMPACTS PERFORMANCE

THE STORY OF A STRUGGLING COMPANY ACHIEVING PROFITABILITY THROUGH CULTURAL TRANSFORMATION

Anita Pugh, Caroline Hipple,
Chris Matthies, Dixon Bartlett

Copyright © 2013 by Anita Pugh,
Caroline Hipple, Chris Matthies, Dixon Bartlett

First Edition – December 2013

ISBN
978-1-4602-1083-3 (Hardcover)
978-1-4602-1081-9 (Paperback)
978-1-4602-1082-6 (eBook)

Produced by:

FriesenPress

Suite 300 – 852 Fort Street
Victoria, BC, Canada V8W 1H8

www.friesenpress.com

Distributed to the trade by The Ingram Book Company
Baker & Taylor

Cover design and graphic design by Steven Davenport

Visit our website at
www.pathwaytoprofit.net

DEDICATION

Stewart H. Brown, Jr.

March 26, 1940 – March 27, 2009

A Pathway to Profit is dedicated to our friend and mentor, Stewart Brown, who embodied the Culture of Caring philosophy instinctively, taught us to expect the best from ourselves, and showed us how to make the most of our opportunities. From him we learned that growing people and growing profits work best when they are intrinsically intertwined. We remember his wisdom that guided our development, respect his financial acumen that gave us a platform for success, and appreciate his sense of fun that allowed us to enjoy it all. In fact, we all loved him in a way few company presidents are ever loved.

Stewart H. Brown, Jr.

We will always be grateful that Stewart's illness did not take him before we were able to tell him that we were writing this book. Libby, his wife and business partner, tells us that our unfinished manuscript was on his bed tray in the weeks prior to his death. Also on that bed tray were hundreds of letters from people who wrote to tell him how his leadership had affected their lives.

On one of Caroline's visits, Stewart shared that he wanted his grandchildren to know that how you treat people makes a difference. When Caroline suggested that he write his thoughts down for them, he replied, "That is what you four are doing!"

Stewart, we hope that this is what you wanted to say.

Advanced Praise for A Pathway to Profit

"Caroline, you and the team have built one heck of a company with one heck of a culture. I'm tempted to say, 'You go, girl,' but I don't have to. You always have and always will."
Raymond Allegrezza, editor in chief, Furniture/Today

"Experience how the key to profitability is a proven employee-driven corporate culture where making money is fun."
Dewey Sadka, author of The Dewey Color System, More Passion, More Power

"It's so exciting to have the secrets of success that I have watched in all four of these authors over the years be quantified in such a usable format for small business owners and managers!"
Ashton Harrison, author of From A.D.D. to CEO

"This interesting and intriguing book seems to make a great deal of sense. A lot of A Pathway to Profit is practical as well as theoretical, and a perusal of the pathway would offer benefits to students of business at all levels."
Littleton Maxwell, business librarian, Robins School of Business, University of Richmond

"I have practiced these leadership principles for more than 25 years, as a business owner and a department manager—they work!"
Margaret Terry, SPHR | chief human resources and administrative officer, Bates Group LLC

"If there's a book you want to read but it hasn't been
written yet, then you must write it."

Toni Morrison, Nobel Prize-winning American author

TABLE OF CONTENTS

INTRODUCTION

Profitability and caring for people are not exclusive, but are actually co-dependent. We believe that the most successful organizations demonstrate a unique ability to marry the seemingly disparate initiatives of expanding profits and developing people. ~Caroline Hipple, President of Storehouse

While this concept merits ink in books and articles, few explain why the people and profit combination works, show how to set it in motion, and give examples from real life that mirror the issues managers face. *A Pathway to Profit* is a step-by-step guidebook for cultural change linking people and profit. We know how to develop this culture because we have been there. Our experience is with real companies, in real jobs where the four authors had front row responsibilities for overall success and profit results.

We won the respect of our industry for the innovative environment we created, a place where people wanted to achieve and consequently produced outstanding results. This interest in our concept and execution encouraged our determination to share our management philosophy through a book. We are all readers and we gained ideas from the fictional business stories with a moral; we adjusted our thinking due to books written by researchers and consultants who chronicle companies and draw conclusions objectively; and we were inspired by the business leaders who tell their own story. In *A Pathway to Profit* we combine the best of these characteristics—the story with the passion of real people, the objective picture of what worked, how we did it and why—and we describe the culture inspired by a management philosophy. Our companies were not easy wins. We experienced multiple hardships, but we will all verify that our culture never failed us.

Each author assumed a different role in developing and implementing the pathway.

Caroline Hipple is the chief architect of the Pathway to Profit process. Combining her instinct and incessant curiosity as to how culture affects profit, Caroline catapulted her career from sales associate through greater levels of responsibility to company president. Her vision, grounded by structure and process, created the opportunity to prove the effectiveness of our management philosophy and forms the basis for this book.

Chris Matthies is the leader of the cultural changes making the pathway possible. As head of stores Chris was the role model for the management philosophy, ensuring that the culture was translated to the customer. Her experience provides practical examples of the pathway in action.

Dixon Bartlett is the link between the culture and brand. Through his role as head of marketing and merchandising, Dixon led the visual manifestation of the culture. His viewpoint lends inspiration throughout the book.

Anita Pugh is the cultural ambassador of the Pathway to Profit. Her calling is to teach managers and associates the individual and relational skills needed to create and perpetuate their vision of an ideal company. Anita is the narrator of our book and from this point is the "I" in storytelling, incorporating the wisdom and experiences of the authors into one voice.

Just as our collective ideas, opinions, and recollections meld into one voice in this book, those same ideas, opinions, and collaboration created the unifying force that reenergized a struggling company. In our story Caroline is the leader, creating the strategy and setting the course. Dixon shapes the visual image—the brand—for both the public and the internal teams. Chris is the manager, ensuring that the sales team and associates support the strategy and become a part of the brand visualization. My role is to teach managers and associates how to build this new culture where personal growth becomes profitable growth.

Although we speak through one narrator, there are also individual thoughts that we have elected to highlight for our readers. The font will be different, the author's name will follow the thought, and the idea will be relevant to the narrative.

Immediately following this introduction, we explain the foundation for the Pathway to Profit management philosophy and how we learned to build a culture. The remainder of the book is devoted to the pathway and how we used the process to revitalize a company.

We cover a strategic overview, describe a recommended architecture on which to build the culture in a company, and present a guide for developing managers by teaching the leadership skills necessary to ensure the associates' willing participation. The chapters follow the pathway. Part 1 of the Pathway to Profit includes chapters 1 - 4 and explains how to build the architectural structure; Part 2 includes chapters 5 – 6 and explains how to build the culture by developing the associates; and Part 3, chapter 7, demonstrates how to maintain the process.

We share the theories as a foundation and that's important, but we also give practical techniques, the "how-to" so that all managers can apply these principles at the level that is right for them.

To explain our concept we share stories from two companies. The first is a start-up company, This End Up, which began modestly with one store and grew to 253 locations, becoming number 19 in the top 100 furniture retailers. Our second company, Storehouse, had been a tired but venerable brand when we transformed it from double-digit loss to profit, becoming number 42 in the top 100 furniture retailers.

What did these two companies have in common? A management team dedicated to a customer-, employee-, and profit-centric management philosophy.

We have seen how leadership decisions can impact people and profits in good times and difficult times. Although our experience happened to take place in two retail furniture companies, concepts here can apply in any organization or group. Because there were thousands of other players in these two companies, we sprinkle the text with their thoughts. As we received their comments, we noticed that they didn't talk much about furniture, but gave a picture of the culture we all built together, how it enhanced their perception of leadership, and changed their lives.

> **What I have learned will stay with me forever. I am better professionally and personally for having lived [this] experience. ~Rich Scarfo, Storehouse**

At the time we are writing this book the global economy suffers unprecedented losses as nations, companies, and individuals experience the most challenging economic crisis in 80 years. People are buffeted by a storm they cannot see, cannot understand, and are powerless to control. Many businesses must be more productive at the same time they are reducing their workforces. This is the new normal.

As leaders of businesses in times of uncertainty, we are forced to grow profits in more creative ways than most of us have previously experienced. While we do not downplay the appeal of generous compensation, comprehensive benefits, award trips and other perks, it may not be possible to guarantee our place in the market by simply spending money. Money does not always guarantee loyalty. In the new norm of the workplace another currency, a cultural currency, must be leveraged.

The cultural currency we share is one that you print yourself, requiring no bank loan, no line-of-credit, no bailout request. The downside of using this currency is minimal; the upside is unlimited. Creating and capitalizing on cultural currency does no harm, and it has the potential to enhance associates' professional and personal lives, transform a company into an employer of choice, enrich the leader's job enjoyment, and blaze a pathway to profit.

We are well aware that a successful company builds a brand, guards its financial health, offers an in-demand product or service, creates an efficient way to get the product or service to the customer, and remains ahead of the competition in every discipline. While we touch on these requirements, our book focuses on the relationships in an organization that allow it to maximize the potential of brand, financial health, product, service, and logistics.

Any organization can take advantage of cultural power. Our system works in large and small companies. It works in good economic times and bad. It works with employees of all ages. It works in the Sunshine Belt and the Snow Belt. It works for businesses, non-profits, schools, and families; in fact, it works for any group that has a leader and team members.

How did we first learn to build the culture of a company? We were fortunate to be employed by This End Up, a small furniture retail chain led by Stewart Brown, an enlightened leader with ideas that were ahead of his time. He introduced us to his management philosophy and we watched him make it work for financial gain and employee enrichment. We learned, side-by-side, how to create a unique business environment that attracts people who work together for company results and individual achievement. We began to understand that these two concepts are not mutually exclusive. Furthermore, we discovered that the key to profitability lay directly in the relationships between the manager and associates within the company, and with customers. We knew that this was a sustainable culture because we managed to grow it for twenty-five years.

By the time I joined This End Up, it had been in business for five years. Caroline and Dixon had been there since year two, and Chris joined us in time for our tenth anniversary. The culture was in its formative stage. I worked in the school system, so had a summer free. A neighbor asked me to replace her at This End Up while she took a two-week vacation. I stayed for 21 years. Why? I loved being there. And I wasn't the only person swept away by the experience of working in an environment that valued my contribution and encouraged me to grow. At This End Up we discovered the secret to an enticing work environment. As we tell the story, we distill and define the culture's ingredients that made people want to be a part of it.

No small element of the charm of This End Up is the rags-to-riches story of how the company began. Never underestimate the appeal of a good story.

THE FOUNDATION FOR THE PATHWAY TO PROFIT

How We Learned to Build a Culture

"[Business] should organize from the customer backwards and
be about the people who make the company work."

Stewart H. Brown, Jr., President of This End Up

THIS END UP

Through our experiences at This End Up we learned that empowered individuals, within a culture that focuses on results, create profit because there is a mutual alignment between personal goals and company goals. ~Caroline

This End Up was the brainchild of Steve Robertson and Randy Ward, two graduates of North Carolina State University who had more fun than stellar financial results in their first few years after college. Upon graduation Steve went off to pursue his love of sailing and travel, and only returned home to regroup. Randy started a roofing company, although not a very successful one. Randy hired Steve to help him with his last job before the company folded, and after completing the job the crew threw a party to celebrate the company's demise. The next day they looked with dismay around Randy's apartment because the only things left standing were the sturdy shipping crates packed with Steve's worldly goods. This destruction truly signified the end of a stage of life. But endings can give rise to creativity, just as this ending did. These were enterprising young men, drawing upon their educational background in product design and textiles, as they tore apart those shipping crates and built a sofa frame. Then, using the cushions they rescued from Randy's sofa, they created a new furniture design. So simple, yet so right for the times. Certainly this sofa was a little rough. Real furniture manufacturers were using hardwood, meticulously sanded, stained, hand rubbed, and polished. Steve and Randy created their revolutionary new design by sanding the pine boards from a packing crate, then combining the frame with the remnants of Randy's trashed sofa cushions thrown in for comfort.

About the only thing going for this new furniture piece was that it seemed pretty much indestructible. No one gazing at this humble sofa would have exclaimed, "This is going to make your fortune!" However, the sofa fit their lifestyles. They later described it as "Furniture You Can Put Your Feet On®." As it turned out, other people were looking for indestructible furniture as well. Problem solved—indestructible furniture with a simple and appealing design.

When friends started asking them to build custom sofas, Steve and Randy decided there might be some money in the idea, so they bought some pine and built several different pieces, then started taking their samples to the Raleigh flea market. There they took orders on Saturday, made the products in a friend's garage during the week, delivered the pieces, and went back to the flea market again the next weekend. Hard work and long hours.

Although they were achieving satisfaction from designing and constructing, neither of them enjoyed selling. They just wanted to make it. Interacting with those customers was the hardest work of all. So, they decided they needed someone who liked to deal with people, freeing them to concentrate on designing and building the products.

Steve's sister, Libby Brown, was in Richmond, Virginia, with two small children, a successful husband, and a comfortable suburban life. Unlike most of her neighbors and friends, Libby did have a job, a nine-to-fiver in a bank's human resources department. Steve contacted her to see if she would like to open a store to sell his new furniture design. He recognized that she had a talent that he wasn't interested in developing. His extreme compliment intended to persuade his sister was, in his words, she "could shoot the #@*& with a lamppost!" Although she was skeptical of his ambitions, after all Steve was her younger brother and the product was pretty rustic, Libby agreed to open a store for this furniture they were calling This End Up. For her shop she chose a trendy neighborhood with a mix of retail and lovely early 1900's townhouses being refurbished by young homeowners. It was a powerful combination—Libby's ability to relate to every customer and a funky product that appealed to these young homeowners. In fact, it was so successful that Stewart, Libby's husband, left his stock brokerage career to take on the president's role, bringing his financial, marketing, and unique management skills to help Libby expand the retail business to other cities.

The Brand

This novel idea to make furniture that could be a part of how people actually live appealed to a wider customer base than was at first apparent. The furniture accommodated small children who could run their trucks on the tables. Scratches were easily fixed, if owners wanted to fix them. Teens loved it because there was no more yelling, "Get your feet off the table!" Party givers stopped worrying about water rings when their guests forgot to use the coasters. In short, it took the activities of a family in stride and kept its good looks.

This End Up was an innovative idea whose timing may have been its strongest suit. Just as Steve and Randy were creating this practical, appealing and affordable style, the vast population of 75 million baby boomers was poised to go into the prime furniture buying years. There was nothing like this style on the market. I know because I looked for it. In 1972 I set out shopping for bunk beds for our son's room, searching for a design I had imagined, not one that I had ever seen. When I first saw This End Up bunk beds I knew that this was the furniture I had been seeking seven years earlier and never found.

This End Up rode the tidal wave of trend setting that this influential population generated on every front. Furniture is a life stage purchase, from the first couch, to the Thanksgiving dinner table, the bunk beds when the child turns 6, to furniture that will fit a teenager's life. We burst on the scene just as this engine began to roll and we captured the market. Several factors lined up for us. We met the new interest in natural products, a move away from the plastic of the sixties and the ornate styles favored by the boomers' parents. Our products were solid wood, pioneering in green design because pine is a renewable resource. Perhaps the deciding factor was the sense of humor in its design. Baby boomers wanted a product that expressed their more casual approach to living, and we were ready for them.

Besides their durability and rustic style, the seating pieces were actually quite comfortable due to the high density foam and the ergonomic angle of the seat and back. Crate-style, as it became universally known, had all the lifestyle qualities going for it that were blatantly lacking in the formal furniture of the 1970's. To illustrate its wide product appeal, over the years we had a number of high profile customers, including Stephen Spielberg and both the George Bush families.

By the 1990's This End Up had sold over a billion dollars of this trend-setting furniture. Only a few single case-goods styles have ever reached that lofty billion-dollar mark, making This End Up one of the most successful furniture ventures ever.

Although it was a unique product in furniture land, uniqueness does not last for 25 years. Copycats soon appeared in our cities. Our owners found that even with design patents, products can be slightly modified and sold in a shop right down the street. The copycats not only seized the opportunity to make the product, they tried to duplicate the look of the stores as well. If This End Up tried a new idea, the competition tagged along right behind, copying everything from locating their stores in malls to creating a catalog. We learned that the product could be copied, our stores could be copied, and our catalog could be copied. Why were our customers devoted to us? The real uniqueness turned out to be with the people who made, sold, and delivered the product. The story of This End Up is really their story.

The Working Environment

Incredibly, we attracted talented people to sell a product line that began life as recycled shipping crates. We earned our associates' respect and such devotion that more than one observer referred to us as "like a cult." The source of the magnetic draw began with the owners. Stewart, Libby, Steve, and Randy all contributed to the *esprit de corps* of the fledgling work environment.

The concept of a balance of talent began with the affiliation of these four entrepreneurs. Imagine the dynamics at play. Not only were the four principals very different temperamentally and talent-wise, but also in the mix there were two friends, a husband/wife combination, and a brother/sister combination, plus the brother-in-law connection. Quite likely no business consultant would recommend that they launch a business together, but they learned to combine their strengths. The appreciation of differences emerged from this first group. When they added people to their team, they selected balancing styles. Understanding the value of talent diversity set the stage for a developmental platform focused on profit and people.

Although Steve and Randy built their manufacturing plant using principles from cottage industries, the furniture builders worked at one site. Each carpenter built a piece from start to finish and signed his or her name. Yes, there were women carpenters. And Ph.D. graduates. The independent nature of the work environment attracted them to This End Up. Other manufacturing facilities couldn't buy the loyalty given to This End Up because the carpenters perceived that they controlled their own destiny, they owned the quality of each piece built, and they were free to excel.

I remember my surprise when first visiting the manufacturing facility. Driving along Route 70 between Raleigh and Durham, the entrance to the factory looked like any other North Carolina pine forest. The driveway meandered through the rhododendrons and pine trees, with parking spaces where the trees allowed. Ahead was a rustic one-story building with a front porch that suggested a fiddling contest might entertain at the end of the day. The building looked modest on the outside, but was innovative on the inside, a metaphor for This End Up itself. Steve and Randy started with one factory and eventually built five facilities on the site. These buildings had high ceilings, workstations with tools and wood for the carpenters, and a modern ventilation system. Years later to keep up with demand we built two other plants with a more traditional assembly-line design, but the manufacturing culture began as a one-carpenter/one-piece process.

> One of the things I remember is that Steve and Randy always sat across from each other at one enormous desk. ~Dixon

Meanwhile, in Richmond the retail office moved from a backroom at the original store and relocated to a historic section of the city, where old abandoned warehouse buildings were newly reclaimed to house restaurants, apartments, and offices. In keeping with other buildings in the area, we kept the office design simple and natural. The original wide plank floors and brick walls set the scene. For years our entrance was on one of Richmond's cobblestone alleys. A national company with an address on Exchange Alley was another expression of our brand.

Under Stewart's leadership the retail company grew to over 200 stores and became one of the first furniture retailers to be included in the rising popularity of enclosed malls. In the 1970's and early 1980's the furniture industry in general comprised big box chains or individually owned local "Mom and Pop" stores. This End Up pioneered the small footprint/multiple store concept for furniture stores. Stewart recognized that most furniture buyers are women, so he hired many women in sales and management positions. He always seemed to be looking right when everyone else was looking left. And how right he was. Up to this point women had not played a big role in the furniture industry, and in the 1970's and 1980's women were hungry for leadership opportunities. They challenged him as he challenged them and together their energy created unprecedented profits. Understanding the importance of customer satisfaction, Stewart insisted that we control the entire process, making our delivery department critical to our success. We manufactured, we sold, and we delivered—vertical integration at its most productive.

This little company with its little stores (the average size of a store was 900 square feet) and its basic common sense approach to furniture eventually attracted the attention of a big name in retailing, the Melville Corporation. Although Melville had no experience with selling, manufacturing, or delivering furniture, they were attracted by the profits This End Up generated. As they researched the business, they became fascinated with the culture making those profits possible. Yielding to an offer they couldn't refuse, Steve, Randy, Libby, and Stewart sold to Melville. Steve and Randy left their manufacturing business, but Stewart and Libby stayed on to run This End Up for another five years.

Melville owned large retail companies, including CVS, Marshalls, Kay-Bee Toys, and the footwear departments of all Kmart stores, and the Melville executives saw an opportunity for those retailers to profit from incorporating parts of the cultural environment of This End Up. Unfortunately, that was not to be. The management groups of these larger divisions saw no need to make the personal changes required for a culture change. After all, they were the big guns and we were so small we could be lost in the rounding of financial reporting. What did we have to teach them? Libby and I reminisced about a meeting we attended in which the other human resources managers and development leaders quizzed us about our culture and how it worked. They were polite in their attention and complimentary in their comments, but most didn't leave our session with the commitment to make changes within their own companies. At least one of these big businesses did see the advantage and made an effort, but not realizing that creating this culture is a process, not a project, the management team did not see how it could work in their business. We knew even then that big businesses are able to benefit from a commitment to culture because by this time the world was familiar with the corporate cultural success stories behind Nordstrom and Southwest Airlines.

What made this little company selling crate-style furniture such a magnet for talent and profit?

Stewart Brown's Management Philosophy

The retail culture began with Stewart Brown's management philosophy, a unique blend of common sense and a simple focus, combined with caring for people and financial goals. Until our store roster approached thirty stores, Stewart and Libby's touch could be felt in every store. In addition to their business responsibilities, Stewart was the sales manager and Libby led the sales training, so they were frequently in the stores. The associates felt they knew them—it was like being close to the flame.

As they added stores Stewart chose his leaders carefully, finding managers who also cared about people and financial goals. His interaction with them combined a heady mixture of managerial and fiscal responsibility, with intense self-evaluation, as he encouraged them to study themselves and their business. Many were young, without strong retail experience, but with big personalities. The typical career path was to work in a store, manage a store, then to manage a district. Most had never held a managerial job elsewhere, so what they knew about managing they learned at This End Up. That anomaly worked for us because we didn't have to counteract management habits learned at companies with more traditional hierarchical structures. These managers compensated for their inexperience with their intellectual curiosity, instinct, and determination to make This End Up a company that attracted talented, interesting people who would in turn attract a loyal customer base. And it worked.

Caroline Hipple was one of those young, just out of college managers. Her father was horrified that her expensive education was resulting in managing a store that sold what looked to him like wooden crates with either cushions or rope drawer pulls. With the courage of her convictions, she assured him that this young company was going to be a very special company, an incubator for growth. "Trust me; someday this is going to be a big company." She could already sense the energy and spirit unleashed in the store and in the home office, and recognized the impact of culture on a company. A generator of energy in her own district, Caroline says, "I had received so much attention and development from Stewart and Libby that I knew it to be my responsibility to pass it along to those that I managed."

Dixon Bartlett's career in hotel management took a left turn when he returned from his honeymoon and his wife, a This End Up district manager, faced a crisis in one store at the same time she was opening another. Dixon to the rescue. In the three months he ran the crisis store he broke sales records and became addicted to the quirky little company. Stewart recognized his talent and assigned him responsibility for developing a new branch of the business, selling to commercial establishments.

Eight years later Chris Matthies was restless. A highly organized Navy wife and mother of two young sons, she looked for a "little part-time job to get out of the house." A friend and This End Up customer recommended that she visit our store. When Chris arrived to discuss the job, the store manager was busy with customers. Chris says, "She was having so much fun, it looked like she was hosting a cocktail party and I thought, 'I can do that!'" And she could. She was soon a store manager, then a district manager, and eventually the head of training and development, teaching others to have fun selling.

What was Stewart's secret? What drew us to This End Up and motivated us to drive its success?

> *He had a genuine love of people and they knew it, and his interest in others was combined with a strong profit motive. His recipe created palpable success for all, and that success became a spinning flywheel powered by the culture. ~Caroline*

Selecting from the myriad of reasons we came and we stayed, we will discuss five concepts in depth:

1. Inclusiveness

2. Listening

3. Fun

4. Honest communication leading to individual growth

5. Orientation to results

1. Inclusiveness

This End Up was clearly the Browns' company and initially none of us had any actual ownership in it. But we felt like we did. The Browns made the strategic decisions and took the financial risks; however, they included the managers in discussions leading to those decisions. Our voices counted. We called it participative management. The participation was at times pretty heated.

One of the most dynamic examples of participative management at This End Up was the hiring of a sales manager, Stewart's role at that time. The district managers talked with Stewart about the possibility of adding a position to lead their team. We don't know if he was surprised, or whether he had been thinking that the business needed a sales manager position. True to his nature, he allowed their input and agreed. Knowing that they had a voice in the business, they "owned" their districts and renewed their determination that this new reporting structure would make the company even more successful.

> *Being an active participant in the creation of a company is powerful currency. ~Caroline*

Setting the environment for this level of participation resulted in good ideas, guaranteed buy-in and retention of motivated talent.

We were always aware that Stewart was the president and an owner of This End Up, but his manner made him one of us, on our team; and in minimizing his "boss" persona, he gave us responsibility for our own success. Even when he was engaging us in difficult discussions, he managed to be effective without ever "pulling rank." Stewart and Libby were well aware of the big blinking sign ever present over their heads that shouted, "Owner!" so they consciously worked to be a part of us—sitting on the floor with the group, offering a beer at the end of the day. Libby even took her turn fixing lunch. I have to admit that Stewart was not on the regular lunch duty schedule, but he could grill a mean burger on those days we took the grill out in the alley. If they were in the office, they were a part of the lunch bunch. These acts made them accessible. In order for the company to grow, our managers would need to duplicate this level of participation throughout the country.

As we increased the number of stores we realized that culture was at the core of our success. While the company expanded along the East Coast it was becoming more difficult for Stewart and Libby to influence every associate at every location. We were poised to launch stores in the Midwest, as well as further expansion in our existing states. Inclusiveness felt really good when we were the ones being included by the owners of the business; however, if all managers did not practice inclusiveness, the concept would stop and would not create the environment throughout the company.

We referred to our company as being geographically challenged. The attitude and skill of the location manager set the environment experienced by associates and customers. Some cities had several stores, but many stores were alone in a city. We faced the challenge of creating culture-savvy district managers, so that every associate could understand the behavior that created the environment they enjoyed, and every customer could feel the benefit of that environment. We needed a definition of our culture to assure that every associate understood the principles important to This End Up. But, what were those principles?

Influenced by Tom Peters and Robert Waterman's bestseller, *In Search of Excellence*, companies across America rushed to create principles that would take their organizations from ordinary to excellent. This End Up had achieved a state of excellence, but we had never analyzed just what had shaped our success. The Browns saw an opportunity to include the management team in solving our pressing problem of maintaining the culture in the face of expansion. At a district manager meeting Stewart and Libby approached the group about delineating the concepts that made This End Up a profitable business and a place where people wanted to work. The managers read *In Search of Excellence* and came back prepared to hammer out the essence of This End Up. A spirited discussion ensued, but at the end of the meeting the group had agreed on ten concepts that became the Shared Values and would constitute the guidelines for managing, making decisions, and running the company.

I sought to include two additions to our list that you won't find named: trust and mutual respect. The group determined that those concepts were implied as we managed our company according to our Shared Values, and I think those principles were the foundation that made the other values work. ~Caroline

An important byproduct of the creation of the Shared Values resulted from the participation process. Inclusion solidified the conviction of those managers that they were important in the strategy of running the company. We began to live the "IWWCW" solution to issues—In What Way Can We...?

The aspect of . . . culture that had the most impact . . . would be the Shared Values. They were very simple, but when you live your life applying them they are very powerful. This was true for my business career as well as personal life. ~Jayne Boyd, This End Up

For me it was the culture of caring and living the Shared Values every day. I still to this day remember all 10 of them. ~John Paladino, This End Up

---

This End Up Shared Values

Maximize Sales
Happy Customers
Individual Growth
Honest Communication
Participative Management
Teamwork
Results Oriented
Flexibility
Minimal Red Tape
Commitment to Excellence

Another way Stewart included us was very subtle. He had the carpenters build a large square table for his office and he used the table as his desk. So, when we went into his office to meet with him we did not sit in the usual chairs on the other side of the desk that identifies and defines the boss. We joined Stewart at his working table. We were a part of his team, not his subjects, and that inclusiveness spawns a difference in motivation that is ever present, even if not stated.

2. Listening

Stewart managed his business by listening to others' ideas and opinions. I remember being in the office late in the evening or on a holiday morning and having Stewart plop himself down in a chair in my office asking, "Tell me what's going on." And he didn't leave until he had learned something to help him improve the company. This unplanned exchange trained me to look for improvement opportunities, the nuggets. Always in touch with the emotional heartbeat of the company, he was a master at "managing by walking around." His eye never wavered from the financial health of the company, but he knew that people who were focused on the business were the driving force creating those numbers.

One reason that he was such a good listener is that he had enormous self-control. His self- confidence prompted him to ask probing questions and allow the answers to fall as they were given. In fact, if he wasn't getting all sides expressed, he might argue the other side of an issue, just to evoke thinking. Or, he would allow a long pause, until true feelings were voiced. Or, he might answer a question with a question. He introduced us to the concept that saying, "No" indicates that you have closed your mind and are no longer listening.

When he offered me the opportunity to head the human resources function, I couldn't have given him a good definition of human resources. I, on the other hand, knew that I could do it due to his confidence in me. He gave me the job because he thought I had a good insight into people and what makes them want to contribute. Thus our human resources department was always focused on how to make people and our company successful. Stewart and I both understood that people announce their attitudes, their strengths and areas for development, if we only know how to watch and listen.

I have a very personal story about Stewart that illustrates the commitment he had to the people who worked with him, above and beyond what would be expected from the owner of a company. Stewart and I were in his office having a heated discussion about something that I don't even remember, but I must have felt some passion, because I became very frustrated and started to do something I rarely do and dislike in myself, especially in a business setting—I was about to cry. I got up abruptly and said that we'd have to continue this later, then walked across the hall to my office and closed the door. No sooner than I had my tissue in place, there came a knock on the door, then Stewart's head peeked in. "I'll have to talk about it later," I said, becoming a bit more annoyed that he wouldn't leave me alone to my emotion. He said, "Let's get through it now." And we did. I cried and he cried and we worked it out. Never had anyone been willing to wade through emotion with me. For me it was the ultimate proof of his commitment. It was the deposit in my emotional bank account that guaranteed he could never be overdrawn.

Stewart was willing to expose his vulnerability to encourage others to share problems. In the sharing came the solutions because he knew how to listen.

The team in the stores became accustomed to Stewart's interest in what was going on with their businesses, but for a new person, it was a bit of a shock to answer the phone and find the company president on the other end of the line.

I had been a store manager about 6 months when I answered the phone to hear Stewart saying, "I hear you have a competitive order you are trying to close." He was calling to brainstorm strategies for negotiating. I was flabbergasted for a number of reasons: this was the company president calling, he knew my name, he was familiar with all the circumstances about the order and he was taking time out of his busy day to coach me! I can't remember anything about the actual transaction, but I fondly remember that Stewart Brown gave me my first lesson in negotiating. He was also giving me a lesson in leadership, although it would be a few years before I understood his subtle approach. ~Chris

3. Fun

Stewart's belief was that if you were not having fun on the job, you should be doing something else; that we all spend too much time at work for us not to enjoy it. Fun could be a party, a good joke, a great story, a challenging work assignment, or the realization of a job well done.

Stewart and Libby were in their element hosting a party. Here they practiced the inclusiveness that endeared them to their team. Never ones to take themselves too seriously, they put everyone else at ease and this gift was an important lesson for all of us.

Although Stewart had sharp critical and analytical skills, when he was working with people he often downplayed those skills to encourage his team to make things happen. He wanted us to be creative, even if the process was whacky. Whacky ideas often worked and certainly caused people to consider something new. Fun also centered around having a good sales month, witnessing the growth of one of the associates, knowing that a task was done well, and receiving recognition from a customer. The ultimate serious fun came from getting recognition from Stewart, which was not lavishly bestowed, so that when it came it was treasured.

All retail managers, distribution managers, and drivers attended our annual meeting. Here we combined a celebration of the year's results and recognition of outstanding individual achievements with the laughter and party that cemented commitment to each other. It was a magical event.

Stewart knew that happy people are more productive and tend to stay with a company longer. Despite retail's typically rapid turnover, a veteran staff is an asset for success in furniture retail. Libby became the master teacher of how to have fun with the customers in the store. Because of our store size, we often had only one associate in the store at a time, so it was important that the associate's fun come from interaction with customers. What an unusual concept in furniture retail—the job in the store was to have fun with customers while selling.

> *There was scant sales training when I started, but I still remember*
> *Libby's suggestion to ask myself two questions after all customers:*
> *1. Did I put a smile on their faces?*
> *2. Did I elevate their mood?*
> *~Dixon*

> *When I first visited the store I had never seen anything like it. The store*
> *manager treated the customers like they were part of her circle of*
> *friends. A man came in with new shoes and we had shoes and tissue*
> *paper all over the place as we admired his purchases. ~Chris*

Years later, after Stewart and Libby were gone, we were reeling from having had a cultural misfit at the helm of our sales organization. We so valued our relationships with our customers that we knew we needed an infusion of fun in the stores. We called six of our former store managers and district managers who were outstanding energy givers and asked them to spend some days in our stores, just demonstrating how to have fun with customers and thereby boost sales. I personally called three of these women and they all agreed enthusiastically, and not one of them asked me if they were being paid.

> *Fun is possible when we have the right people in the right places in our*
> *company. Work is fun when we are unleashing our unique talents. Our*
> *concentration of matching skills and experience to job needs allowed*
> *us to be less rule-oriented. ~Caroline*

4. Honest communication leading to individual growth

Stewart gave honest feedback. Sometimes positive results were acknowledged and it felt good; sometimes results were less than required and that didn't always feel good. He allowed us to grow no less than we expected of ourselves. Honest feedback may sound easy, but the delivery makes the difference between deflating the effort and finding the solution. Any manager can deliver a scathing evaluation of an employee's work, but few can make the employee feel gratitude for the guidance. Stewart could see and discuss the problem without making the other person feel like the problem. Under his leadership we pushed ourselves beyond our comfort zones. The result was growth, as might be expected. However, what might not be as apparent was that his nudge led to our loyalty. The more invested he was in the growth of a member of his team the more he focused on honest communication. His belief that happiness at work could exist only in an environment of individual growth drove his commitment to each of us.

Being willing and able to give honest communication was one of the more difficult practices that our managers learned. The ability to hold up the mirror for associates in such a positive fashion that they appreciate the reflection, and are willing to be introspective about the observation, requires a trusting relationship and an environment where honest communication is customary and expected. Honest communication is not easy to do, and not a natural skill for most people. We watched and learned from Stewart.

> **My job at [This End Up] was by far the best job I've ever had because I learned so much about business/managing and myself. I'd give anything to work in a [This End Up] environment once again. I still appreciate the confidence and support that Stewart and Libby gave me, and all that I learned from everyone at [This End Up.] ~Margaret Breuer, This End Up and Storehouse**

At no time was honest communication more important than when a person was not working out in a job. Stewart was convinced that a good manager would never have to fire anyone. He believed that if there were a constant exchange of honest communication, both parties would either resolve issues or one would change jobs. I happen to think that "never" having to fire anyone is a lofty goal, but I do agree that a good manager rarely has to fire anyone.

Stewart gave people a chance to improve, knowing that success in learning and growth in job skills comes at different stages for different people. His tendency to sleep on it, rather than make a hasty decision, kick-started many careers. He focused on other people's success, yet was not personally threatened by their failure. Giving people a chance to succeed had two important byproducts—they were motivated to do their best, and the rest of the organization watched, knowing that he would do the same for us.

Through Stewart's example we were able to retain those associates who were nourished by the culture and made significant contribution to the company. We learned to counsel those who were not thriving in the culture. Our experience was that when the culture is strong enough, it develops its own retention and rejection character and those who don't subscribe usually choose to leave.

A positive example of honest communication occurred with Stewart and one of the first This End Up managers. She had started working in a store and was an amazing salesperson, at ease with every customer. Having succeeded in sales, she became a store manager, then a district manager. As she moved farther from the customer and more into achieving results through others, her record of success began to falter. Because he cared about her as well as the business, he was willing to talk with her about what he observed. Stewart helped her to see that managing people was not bringing her satisfaction. It was not that she was unable to manage people; it was just not her primary interest. Although she subscribed to the culture, her career path was outside the fledgling company she had helped to launch. She elected to leave and soon became a successful stockbroker. Her performance was dependent on her relationships with her customers, so that her talent created her success. She remained a friend of This End Up and an admirer of the insight Stewart brought to her career.

Stewart recognized Caroline's talent and held the mirror up to her so that she could grow. He helped her identify her weaknesses as opportunities and transform them into strengths. Did she always feel gratitude for his insight? To be perfectly honest, sometimes this headstrong young woman's first emotion was possibly denial rather than gratitude, but she listened and learned to act on his counsel. Repeated success taught her to welcome the lessons. When she became president of our next company, it was to Stewart she went for honest communication.

5. Orientation to results

Trying hard is important, but if the goal is profit, even the most ardent endeavor isn't enough unless financial results are forthcoming. Stewart and the management team were committed to getting results. Stewart attacked the profit margin from every angle.

Our focus was a happy customer, not just a satisfied customer. We enjoyed an unprecedented 40% return customer rate and much of our new business success came through word of mouth. Customers received such outstanding service in our stores that they came back again and again, and they told their friends and family about us. The customers' children were sure that our managers lived in the stores, "See mommy, I told you she lives there!" The associates in our stores got to know their customers. Their sales soared. The result was a healthy income.

Our simple product line allowed us to focus on building skills in salesmanship and sales management. Led company-wide by Libby Brown, enormous time and resources were given to sales development. In the stores we taught our associates to guide the interaction with customers and create such a bond that it was comfortable to say, "Ask for me." or "Have you had a positive experience?" or "Would you recommend us to a friend?" From such customer relationships we built our business. Happy customers driving sales.

Income is not enough for healthy business results. Stewart was a fanatic about conserving the hard-earned cash the customers paid us. The company paid its own way, no debt. That meant serious conservation of resources. Stewart and the sales team set up the early stores themselves, lining bare walls with reed fencing. No cash registers, no computers, no cash wrap counters, and sometimes no back-rooms. The store layout was a study of simplicity. The furniture served as fixtures and the people added the sparkle. Each store displayed a sampling of the product. Customers placed orders for future delivery based on samples in the stores, much like open-stock china. Larger stores could show every product; smaller stores relied partially on pictures, and associates learned to sell products not shown. Supplies were carefully monitored. Every penny was duly pinched twice before it was spent. I have to admit that Stewart took some grief due to the way he managed the financial health of the company, but he took the ribbing in good humor and continued to be a strict steward of a profitable business and its resources.

While Stewart demonstrated his results orientation, others in the company showed their commitment in their own realms. Libby recognized the value of a good story and led the drive in enriching the company lore. She loved a funny story and nobody told it better than she did. But she also promoted the service stories that demonstrated our commitment to customers. We learned the value of telling stories at the same time we learned the value of the commitment to results.

At every big meeting, Sara Flemer Simpson, the first sales manager, used her precious minutes in front of the group to share positive customer comments she had received. I have to admit that in the beginning I didn't understand why she read all those letters. As I witnessed more of the subtle building blocks of this culture I did eventually comprehend. To Sara the customer was more important than the product and the better we knew the customer, the more product we would sell. She was teaching us that every sale is a person's story. Of course, she was evaluated on the final sales figure, but she was smart enough to know that the people attending the meeting would produce better sales numbers if they knew their customers and could identify what made them happy.

There were so many stories about commitment that we added an annual award to honor people who went above and beyond in their commitment to results. Their stories were read to the entire management group and they were invited to the stage to sit in director's chairs individually stenciled with their names. The recipients took their chairs to their locations, proudly displayed for their coworkers. Winning the "chair award" became an effective way to recognize achievement because it was available to anyone who demonstrated outstanding commitment.

Some of the most amazing stories were about our home delivery drivers. One driver and helper team was delivering to a beach house on an island. They rode the ferry across and prepared to drive the truck to the customer's house. The problem soon became apparent. There was no road. Unwilling to compromise on the results, they carried the furniture piece by piece a mile up the beach to the customer's home and placed it carefully in the second-floor rooms. No one would have expected them to lug those heavy pieces in the sand. To those drivers bringing the furniture back on the truck would have been unacceptable. They took their results seriously and we celebrated their commitment.

A store manager learned sign language so that she could communicate with a hearing-impaired customer.

One holiday season we sold an assemble-it-yourself dollhouse. A customer was excited about giving her child the dollhouse, but she was simply unable to put it together. The store manager assembled the dollhouse, painted it, and delivered it on Christmas Eve.

Picture this: Our district manager was at the reception just after her own wedding when she received a phone call about her business. There she stood, in her beautiful bridal gown, talking her team through the problem. It was her district, her managers had all attended the wedding, and she was fully committed to working through the problem with the team in the store.

There are a thousand stories.

Evergreen Ideas That Grew in this Culture

In many ways one of the greatest satisfactions was a sense that you controlled your own environment and your efforts directly affected the profit of the company. ~Dixon

One result of participative management is that all the good ideas for our company did not come from Stewart or Libby. They encouraged their managers to be themselves, to bring their personalities to work as they interacted with associates and customers. When we brainstormed cultural norms practiced at This End Up we were astonished at the number of concepts that we had integrated into our approach to leadership. We believe that everyone can find a nugget of wisdom in this list.

- ✓ It's not about the product, but the people who use it.

- ✓ Never say "No" the first time.

- ✓ Get off perfection and get on with the job.

- ✓ Buy time to sift through what is important.

- ✓ Use pauses to get the other person talking.

- ✓ Don't make a decision until you have to. (That one really was Stewart's!)

- ✓ Work on one area of personal development at a time.

- ✓ To get clarification, answer a question with a question.

- ✓ Ready, fire, aim works if you are not afraid of uncertainty.

- ✓ Make education participant-centered.

- ✓ Counterbalance talents, experiences, and temperaments when creating a team.

- ✓ Drill down until you understand the root cause of the problem.

✓ Honest communication can build trust; tell the truth no matter how difficult; it is an investment in the future.

✓ Turning a problem back to the problem-bearer for resolution is giving a gift that creates confidence.

✓ Embrace your mistakes, learn from them and try again.

✓ Embrace differences and creativity.

✓ There are different paths to the same result.

✓ People excel in their area of talent.

✓ Expect the best from others and they will deliver it.

✓ A sense of humor is a valuable and useful trait.

✓ Learn to laugh at yourself.

✓ Crying is OK, for men too.

✓ Be accessible; leave your door open literally and figuratively.

✓ Ask, ask, ask instead of tell, tell, tell.

✓ Many problems can be solved by getting to know each other.

✓ This is your company; don't let it screw up!

✓ If you see something wrong, get a fix going.

✓ "It's not my job" is not an option.

✓ Toggle the loose/tight property of independence and instruction.

✓ Manage the gray when the situation is neither right nor wrong.

✓ Use a light touch with heavy subjects.

✓ Empower decision-making at the closest point to the issue.

✓ Show up, listen, laugh lots.

✓ Work can be fun.

By affording their managers the ability to impact their environment, Stewart and Libby were rewarded with loyalty, profitability, and creativity.

I didn't understand the power of managing in the gray until I worked with Stewart. With the end goal in mind, I learned to set out guide-posts of opportunity and proceeded through the inevitable uncertainty on the way to our success. ~Caroline

One day Stewart and I were having one of our philosophical discussions, this time on the topic of someone being discharged from a company. His comment was, "You could fire me any time you want." I looked at him askance. He was the owner of this company. He was my manager. I had no power to fire him and told him so. He said, "All you have to do is leave and I am essentially fired." We read about presidents who are discharged by the board of directors, but our president realized that his job would not exist without us and viewed himself as working for his associates and the customers.

We were all also very aware that the customer could "fire" us at any time. Stewart turned a tops-down management pyramid upside down. Our company direction came from the customer and those who touched the customer and funneled down to him.

Stewart embodied the best of enlightened self-interest. He understood that if the rest of us succeeded in the realization of our dreams, he would succeed in the realization of his. We did, and he did. As we review our years at This End Up we realize that for us professionally and personally success was a heady experi-ence. We found that winning multiplies winning, and being a part of a winning team is addictive.

When we left This End Up we had to dissect, examine, and document how the management system we dubbed the "Culture of Caring" worked, so that we could apply these profitable principles in building another business.

THE CULTURE OF CARING

The Culture of Caring is a multi-faceted management system that engages employees and unleashes profits, both fiscal and relational. It is a method of management and development in an organization that combines the focus on the positive development of the "human capital" and maximizes bottom-line profit. The Culture of Caring is financially based, but at the same time it is people centered. ~Caroline

The true "hero" of *A Pathway to Profit* is not a person, but a management system. When we told Stewart about the book we were writing to share his management philosophy, he said, "You have a hard job. Your notion of culture change is really swimming upstream. Most companies are not organized around their people, or really their customers. They are often organized around the financials and their product, and the CEO. Don't get me wrong; these are critical. But they miss the point. We should be organized around the customer and the people that make the company work. We have it wrong in America. We should be bottoms up, not tops down. We should organize from the customer backwards and be about the people who make the company work."

This End Up's cultural and financial success spawned the development of our Pathway to Profit, a process

"Culture is what makes the experience of working at one company different than doing the same work at another company."

Peter Sholtes,
The Leader's Handbook

Culture – "The set of values, goals, and practices that characterizes an institution or organization."

Merriam-Webster

allowing us to reproduce our management system in another organization. As we predicted, the culture and the pathway are fundamentally intertwined and implementing our pathway gave rise to the work environment we began to refer to as "The Culture of Caring."

The Culture of Caring? That may sound soft and easy, but I guarantee that it is anything but soft, and it certainly isn't easy. In fact, when we coined the phrase we paused in our concern that people would assume that caring meant a sugarcoated, warm and fuzzy, pushover kind of environment. Our Culture of Caring requires managers to respect enough to develop associates, not just discard them, while requiring associates to maximize their individual potential. We talk about tough growing pains as associates develop through introspection, responsibility, and accountability. In this environment people must consider how their actions affect their teammates, both within the department and in other departments, and the entire organization must genuinely care about customers and company profit.

The Culture of Caring becomes an ever evolving, changing quest to create the working platform that produces profits for investors, a leadership venue for managers, engagement for associates, vendor cooperation, and customer loyalty. Although this environment may use different methods than the traditional boss/employee method, it does not relax accountability and responsibility, and never loses focus on the result. We believe that the Culture of Caring applied in other organizations can change the working world.

> In my time since This End Up I have never found this again. I have searched for it and currently work for a mission based organization, but it is still not [This End Up]. I am not sure that the culture will ever exist again, but I do know that many organizations would benefit from trying. ~Mark Ferraro, This End Up

> When you know that the person who signs your check sincerely cares about you and the business at hand you will do more to make certain that you put forth your very best at all times. ~Kiom Maraschiello, Storehouse

We learned at This End Up that it is more profitable to care. The method we describe taps into the basic needs of people, including the need for belonging and connecting. Tapping in doesn't cost money; but it does cost time and energy.

Today's organizations struggle with employee turnover, low productivity, and changing customer loyalties—all profit eaters. The concept of profitability through culture finds support in The Gallup Organization's research, which suggests that the answer to profit is "engaged employees," employees who care about their customers and their company. The challenge for business leaders becomes—how do we attract the talent, develop them, and keep them?

The importance of culture also finds support from the well-known consumer and corporate research firm, Yankelovich, which keeps tabs on the attitudes of the American public. They name the top three reasons for employee satisfaction:

1. I have a good working relationship with my manager.

2. I have friends at work that I like.

3. I relate to and buy into my company's vision, mission, shared values, and goals.

Employee satisfaction is important because managed wisely it leads to engaged associates. Our own research confirmed the effect of relationship building. As we were writing this book we realized that an overwhelming majority of people who contacted us to comment on the Culture of Caring identified the relationship with their co-workers to be the number one experience they missed in their new jobs. This very connection creates organizational currency.

> I am finally able to approach things more gracefully. The first time I heard my team tell me that they enjoyed working for a caring manager, I almost fell out of my chair!
> –Barbara Gionti, This End Up

Why does the Culture of Caring work? Years of application show that associates want to connect their own motivation to the company's interest. We found that people who are energized and excited about what they are doing are more productive, and they attract others who are also energized, excited, and more productive.

The brilliance of the Culture of Caring resides in the fact that it includes everyone. I have been thoroughly engaged on a day-to-day basis in the companies described in these pages, not an outside observer. I have not been at the top, able to control my company's destiny. In other words, I have been where many of our readers are, a part of a company, feeling ownership, but not necessarily experiencing actual financial ownership. I have been able to impact profits from my position in both the companies we describe. I have witnessed how building a positive company environment not only makes a rewarding place to work, but also that a good company culture impacts profit. I felt a powerful energy knowing that I affected profitability, even though my roles in human resources and training wouldn't appear to be directly related to profits. In this culture each individual has an impact.

A basic premise became clear to us as we practiced the Culture of Caring: giving permission and training to solve issues at each position in the company resulted in good decisions and engaged employees. The top manager is not as effective in solving problems at the middle level as the savvy manager on the scene. Carried further, mid-level managers are not as effective solving customer problems as the well-informed and skilled associate who regularly interacts with the customer. Think about the deli counter at the grocery store. In packaging cold cuts, the person who has permission to correct a mislabeled price indicates the confidence of the store manager and demonstrates the store's focus on the customer. In our experience, being confident of the ability and having permission to influence our own environment builds individual growth and loyalty to company goals. For this powerful engine to hum smoothly, we applied education and empowerment equally.

> **The aspect that had the most impact on me was the ability to use my creativity. The management staff always encouraged everyone to think creatively in order to problem-solve and provide superior customer service. The reason [we were] successful was the fact that new ideas and processes were embraced and when possible implemented. This gave everyone a real connection to the work being done. Also, creativity was rewarded. When a new idea or suggestion was enacted that employee was praised and acknowledged for their efforts. ~Mark Ferraro, This End Up**

> *This culture requires the leaders to show up, listen, laugh, and get engaged. They must be present where the action is, with the customers and those who touch the customers. Leaders must drive education, empowerment, and decision-making down to the closest touch point to the customer. ~Caroline*

Still not convinced this idea has merit? Consider the tales of Southwest Airlines and Nordstrom. What makes them different from their competition is their culture. Although it is a smaller enterprise, the spotlight shines on the World Famous Pike Place Fish Market in Seattle. The employees at Pike Place decided to act like their very ordinary fish market was world famous, and soon it was. What could make a fish market special, other than fresh fish? The culture. L.L. Bean developed a prolific catalog business during a time when other catalogers were losing the struggle to maintain their customer base. This Maine retailer acted on core values, knowing the customers, offering quality products, cheerful and efficient phone service, and a no-questions-asked return policy. These companies validate our focus on culture.

> **Defining corporate values (and the vision of the founders), and using them universally in decision making gives employees confidence to work autonomously. ~Jane Toney, This End Up**

Our Pathway to Profit, organized in an easy-to-understand format, groups the theories, processes, programs, activities and tasks necessary to create an empowered team, the Culture of Caring. This empowered culture produces engaged associates as Gallup describes and satisfies the associate needs that Yankelovich uncovered. While the diagram looks like a funnel, propelling us relentlessly to the end, we must caution that pressing issues may require initiating the process at a point other than the beginning. And the issues along the path may require revisiting the beginning. In a perfect situation we think that the pathway as we have designed it works well. However, its purpose is to be adaptable to a leader's needs. The pathway is an iterative and circuitous process and we found ourselves fast forwarding, or rewinding as needed.

> *The leader must have the vision to get over hurdles. It is not all linear and you have to allow for distractions from the world. ~Caroline*

The first four sections of the pathway explain how to create an organizational architecture for profitable growth. The next two sections explain how to create the culture for company relationships focused on the customer. This pathway's destination is the Culture of Caring, a multi-faceted management system that engages employees and unleashes profits, both fiscal and relational. At the beginning transforming the culture seems to be a daunting endeavor, but once established, it becomes power to the engine that drives business.

How does the company culture ultimately affect profits? Nurturing a culture that empowers associates to create outstanding customer experiences increases repeat customers and word-of-mouth recommendations. In this world of instant communication, customers rate us every day. Our profits depend on their good will.

We didn't find an easy stroll down the pathway. There was no magic moment when everyone shrieked a loud "Aha!" in unison. The breakthrough indicator could be a comment overheard, or a project that moves incredibly smoothly, or a balance sheet that actually balances; but at some point organizations realize, as we did, that the momentum is carrying the company.

> *Our purpose is to demonstrate how empowering individuals has transformational effects on personal fulfillment, organizational enrichment, and profitability. To be competitive, companies must re-examine strategy, pare down to the core, become even more meaningful to customers, reduce expenses . . . AND tap into the hidden treasure of employee empowerment. Energizing employees is a profit driver, not a profit drainer. ~Caroline*

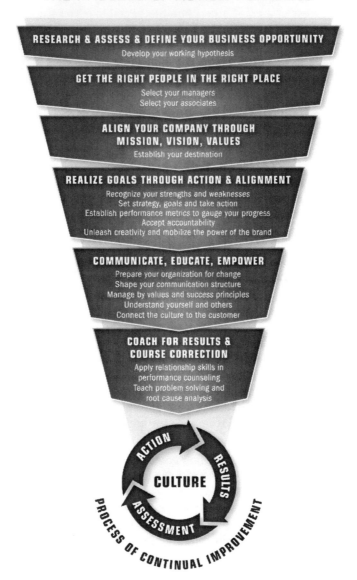

PATHWAY TO PROFIT
THE PROCESS OF ACTION PLANNING

RESEARCH & ASSESS & DEFINE YOUR BUSINESS OPPORTUNITY
Develop your working hypothesis

GET THE RIGHT PEOPLE IN THE RIGHT PLACE
Select your managers
Select your associates

ALIGN YOUR COMPANY THROUGH MISSION, VISION, VALUES
Establish your destination

REALIZE GOALS THROUGH ACTION & ALIGNMENT
Recognize your strengths and weaknesses
Set strategy, goals and take action
Establish performance metrics to gauge your progress
Accept accountability
Unleash creativity and mobilize the power of the brand

COMMUNICATE, EDUCATE, EMPOWER
Prepare your organization for change
Shape your communication structure
Manage by values and success principles
Understand yourself and others
Connect the culture to the customer

COACH FOR RESULTS & COURSE CORRECTION
Apply relationship skills in
performance counseling
Teach problem solving and
root cause analysis

ACTION
RESULTS
CULTURE
ASSESSMENT
PROCESS OF CONTINUAL IMPROVEMENT

FIGURE #1 THE PATHWAY TO PROFIT IS DIVIDED INTO PART 1—CREATING AN ORGANIZATIONAL ARCHITECTURE FOR PROFITABLE GROWTH (STEPS 1-4), PART 2—CREATING THE CULTURE FOR COMPANY RELATIONSHIPS FOCUSED ON THE CUSTOMER (STEPS 5-6), PART 3—THE PROCESS OF CONTINUAL IMPROVEMENT.

PATHWAY TO PROFIT
PART 1

Creating an Organizational Architecture for Profitable Growth

"When your assets walk out of the building each night,
culture is very important."

David Williams, Deloitte Financial Advisory Services CEO

Venturing into the unknown is the challenge

You may be . . .

✓ Seeking a new job

✓ Leading a new company

✓ Revitalizing a company or a department

✓ Improving performance levels

✓ Increasing your customer base

And the question is: Where to start?

CHAPTER 1
Where to Start?

Begin with research, research, research. Identify your customer, your market, your strengths, weaknesses and opportunities. As you create your working hypothesis you will refine your ideas about your core strength, clarify your market position, and ultimately distill your ideas into strategies, goals, and your mission. ~Caroline

While our first story would not have been noteworthy without the influence of Stewart Brown, our next story would not have happened without Caroline Hipple's ability to design a process reproducing the culture that had sustained This End Up's profitability. This chapter tells how she built a plan for our next venture. Her experience gives insight as to how to build a model, whether it is preparing personally or structuring an organization.

Who is this Caroline Hipple? How did this ambitious young college graduate advance her career from sales associate to company president? Why is her story important? By drawing upon her real life experience she was able to build an organizational structure that transformed a company. Caroline always worked at the forward edge of her abilities and was fortunate to find a mentor who was unflinching in his commitment to her personal and professional growth. Caroline credits the combined power of having a great mentor, a practical need to make it happen, the aptitude and willingness to study the underlying principles that could be replicated, and being surrounded by smart colleagues, each with a unique approach to solving problems and gaining success. Hers is the story of resolute talent meeting opportunity and the leadership model that grew from her experience.

Four words that changed my life came one night while I was having dinner with Stewart Brown at the Gadsby's Tavern in Old Town Alexandria. "I believe in you," Stewart said. I was a young store manager for This End Up, and Stewart was recruiting me to go to Chicago to be the district manager for the next district opening. I will never ever forget that feeling or those words. I left that restaurant walking on air. For the first time I felt the inspiration of someone taking an interest in my growth and development and the power of someone painting a picture of success and putting me in it.

Before you can understand that scene, let me tell you how I found This End Up. As a newly minted college graduate in the mid-1970's, I headed to Washington, D.C. to begin my career in the world, armed with the notion I had been taught by my parents and my schools, that I could do anything I strived to do. I hoped to work in the business and people side of an art auction company, using my degree in art history. To pay the rent I took a job as a sales assistant with an investment banking firm. My father was delighted. He was going to have a stock-broker in his future. However, I saw that the leading job for a woman in that organization was a sales assistant with little room for advance-ment. I don't think they saw me as the next VP, but I did.

One particularly difficult day, my phone rang and it was a college mate arranging for a furniture delivery for my boss. The company was This End Up, a new, quirky, cool furniture concept expanding in the Washington area. One of my best college friends had just taken a store manager job in Bethesda. This call came from her boss, also a college friend. I asked if they needed any help on the weekends or in the eve-nings. Of course they did. And six months later I was asked to become a store manager.

Quickly I saw that my opinion counted. Company leaders knew me by name, and they knew my accomplishments. I had good friends at work, people I liked and respected. I was a part of something larger than myself. I was learning about business, sales, marketing, and management. All top reasons people stay with a company.

This brings us back to the Chicago offer and Stewart's electrifying words, "I believe in you." Well, I did not go to Chicago because the next opening turned out to be in Philadelphia. I packed my bags and moved north to develop a district of nine stores. In 1979 what kind of company trusted a 23-year old, just out of college, female district manager? A company with a visionary leader who was an innovator in many ways, including developing women in key management positions. I was long on confidence, but short on real people management experience. This is where Stewart's incredible people focused management changed my life and my career.

The foundation for my ensuing years of success was laid in these three short, somewhat painful and difficult years that we worked together to build the Philadelphia district's success. We worked to grow This End Up and its training and philosophies and culture. And we worked to build and develop my management skills, specifically, people management skills. This was painful for me and probably more painful for Stewart as he held up the mirror. I would defend or fight his notion, then go home, consider it, and by the next day, or the next week, I would be working on it. Step by step I saw vast improvement in my skills and my successes. It took lots of emotional energy and courage for both of us.

I also attended business and marketing classes on sales and management at The Wharton School. I began to watch and evaluate the successful leaders around me, learning to predict the results and hoping to be able to replicate the behaviors that produced the results.

I went on from that Philadelphia post to pioneer the New England district and then the entire West Coast. All in all I spent my first 13 years opening and managing stores and learning the ins and outs of store operations, and what makes customers happy. Along the way, I had discovered a passion for marketing and merchandising, so in a quite unusual move I came in from the field to the home office to manage our marketing and merchandising efforts. Thanks again to Stewart and This End Up for taking a risk on me. Eventually, I combined all of my experience and became the executive vice president in charge of the front end of the business, managing sales, marketing, and merchandising.

This story seems to be about my experience, but it is really about how this culture shaped me. When I realized what I was gaining and the incredible results my team was achieving, it inspired me to want to give forward so that the culture could continue for others. It became the key motivation for my work life. To fulfill that need to give forward, I needed to understand what made it work.

Other events triggered the need to understand the elements of culture. Stewart and Libby were preparing to leave when they brought me into the home office to lead the marketing and merchandising departments. I was no longer a direct influence in the sales force. Dixon also

*left the field for a position in the home office. After Stewart and Libby
left, the leadership of our sales team rested in a new vice president of
stores from outside the company. His style was the antithesis of our
culture and he quickly sought to remold the sales team. Our challenge
was to preserve our profitable culture without Stewart to guide us, and
with a powerful force against us. Chris came into the office to lead the
training and development that was essential to preserving our success.
Anita and I spent many late evenings in what seemed to be rambling
conversations, but became our foundation for observing, analyzing,
and codifying the elements that made our culture work. Our objective
was to build a structure that could withstand adversity. It was the
understanding of this structure that gave me the courage of my convictions that a Culture of Caring was possible to create, and that it could
be an avenue to profit through people in other companies. ~Caroline*

Develop Your Working Hypothesis

When Caroline left This End Up she wanted another opportunity to grow a business that balanced the developmental needs of people and the profit needs of
a company, using the two concepts to strengthen each other. Her first step was
to create a working hypothesis, the preliminary step to crystallizing a vision.
A vision may be a new job, a more cohesive department, a rejuvenated small
business, a turnaround financial picture, improving performance, or strengthening the customer base. Caroline's vision was a new company.

Find What's in It for You

In defining a new challenge, one of the first questions to ask may come as a
surprise: What's in this for me? We acknowledge that for people to do their
best, their efforts must tie to their own self-interest. While many observers and
participants saw the culture of our two companies as being the ultimate in a
work environment (and it was), it was also a source of enlightened self-interest.

What is enlightened self-interest? Each individual determines self-interest
through life-long introspection, through personal awareness of strengths and
weaknesses, and through identifying a personal mission and vision. Aligning
personal goals with the company's goals promises a combination for success.

*I was so lucky to have had Stewart Brown, the founder of This End
Up, as my mentor and I remembered his advice: "Think about how
a particular action affects you." I learned to consider the principle of
using enlightened self-interest. I would be much more effective if the
engagement in the challenge also met my needs. ~Caroline*

Organize Your Research

Where to start? As Caroline planned the path to launching a new company, her attempt to build a working hypothesis took her through a fog of uncertainty, and only her patience and tenacity in gathering information allowed her to sort it into a pattern. Overwhelming goals become more possible when divided into projects. Although mileposts will be different for every endeavor, her mileposts illustrate the concept.

- ✓ Meeting with companies within the industry. She contacted companies she admired and discussed their approaches to business success.

- ✓ Touring retail around the world. She concentrated her research in Europe, especially in the style-setting environs of Paris and London.

- ✓ Exploring the Internet phenomenon. At the time the furniture industry was not innovative in marketing products online.

- ✓ Asking questions. She queried every source for information: bankers, investors, entrepreneurs, style mavens, and large and small retailers.

- ✓ Challenging assumptions. This required some courage, and not a little audacity, because the furniture industry was particularly strong at assuming the current strategy was the best strategy.

- ✓ Keeping a journal with a detailed list of potential goals. Maintaining her focus on goals prevented her research from evolving into chasing dreams.

- ✓ Editing concepts, eliminating and adding while exploring projects. Although it took discipline to edit, she knew that too many possibilities could lead to a mental roadblock.

As a result of the external research process, she began to get a more comprehensive view of the market.

Consider the Customer

As a visionary leader Caroline always saw the market as it could be, not content to accept it as it appeared. This ability to envision drove her market research, starting with the customer. Every business or service has a customer and success hinges on how the customer reacts. Realizing that customers would drive profits, Caroline developed goals from the customer back. Minor changes to the questions below will allow most organizations to assess their customer focus.

Her questions for analyzing the market:

✓ Who is the key customer?

✓ What do customers need?

✓ How are competitors satisfying customers' needs?

✓ What do customers want?

✓ How does the company interact with customers?

✓ How does the company build a desirable brand?

✓ What is the market lacking?

✓ What are the strengths of the market?

✓ What would be the organization's reason for being?

✓ How would the company be unique?

A company's brand cannot exist without impacting its culture and vice versa. Thus we include the questions Caroline asked herself as she looked for the energy in the market, both in the United States and Europe, to determine what was attracting customers.

✓ Who are the customers who are drawn to the stores?

✓ What information can be surmised from the characteristics of sales people and the quality of their interaction with customers?

✓ How does visual presentation in stores exhibit energy?

✓ How effective is product mix?

✓ What is available in other countries but has not yet entered the U.S. market?

✓ How are products selected, designed, and sourced?

✓ What do graphics and advertising look like?

Through this research the merchandising picture for a new company began to emerge.

The visual aspects of brand and culture reflect each other. ~Dixon

The next avenue for research focuses on identifying sales channels, customer transaction points, and service model. Caroline approached this question from the customer's viewpoint:

- ✓ How do they get a product or service?

- ✓ How does a company make it the most convenient and compelling experience for the customer?

- ✓ How does technology assist the customer?

In Caroline's quest, store locations would be a logical first step, but her experience had also taught her that a catalog business was popular with customers, and profitable. And, although in the year 2000 the furniture industry had not become a big player in the Internet, Caroline saw that Internet could reach customers who would never see a store or receive a catalog. Her vision included giving customers a choice of channels: store visit, catalog and phone order, and interactive Internet, all with the same customer-focused service.

Through this research a clear picture of an attainable business model emerged to support her vision of a profitable company with an empowered culture. Why did she do this research before she had an opportunity? The vision may be general, it may be written in pencil, but a leader needs a sense of direction to be effective.

Outline Your Business Model

We are not suggesting this creation of a business model took place in a boardroom with big leather seats, attorneys to ensure that the wording was advantageous, and financial advisors to test the viability of the plan. We are talking about an airplane over the Atlantic, with Caroline and Dixon scribbling notes and lists on legal pads. Other venues may be as simple as a restaurant with lists on a napkin.

During this flight Caroline and Dixon turned their attention to internal organization. Pulling from their experience of building a customer-focused service team, they analyzed the process of shaping the working culture that would encircle customers, products, and service.

Examples of internal questions to ponder:

- ✓ Who are we?

- ✓ What will we be?

- ✓ What is our mission?

- ✓ How do we accomplish our mission?

✓ What do we do well?

✓ What are our opportunities for change?

Their passage through this research led them to their business model. The industry may be different, the end result may be different, opportunities may be different, but the process by which leaders find their answers lies in the questions they ask and the answers they find.

With Dixon's help on that trans-Atlantic flight, Caroline honed their information into a business model.

✓ A limited number of stores to establish a strong culture before expanding

✓ The buying power of a large company

✓ A critical mass to take advantage of pricing

✓ A specialty store format

✓ High customer service

✓ Ability to create a multi-channel platform

✓ Special order program

The research was done; the model was on paper; and Caroline's attention turned inward to evaluate her ability to lead this envisioned organization.

I was following my process with the goal that I would define a vision within six months, but I was open to learning as I moved down the path with confidence that the process would lead me to a clear vision. Which it did. ~Caroline

Assess Your Leadership Skills

I saw how Stewart's people-centered approach allowed him to shape and balance his team of contrasting players, always with an appreciation of our differing gifts. For instance, when we had disagreements between managers, he always insisted that we see the situation from the other person's point of view and that we work it out ourselves. This precipitated the development of strong relationships between individual managers and their departments.

A leader must be willing to seek diversity, and then unite the team to a common purpose, to watch each other's backs, and to put the company's best interest at the forefront of decision-making. A good leader must have an appreciation for the differences and talents of the individual team members and the ability to forge a functional group capitalizing on the differences.

A team always has a leader and the leader always has an impact on the dynamics of the team. It is impossible to eliminate that phenomenon. A good leader must understand his or her impact on the team, and I was determined to be a good leader.

I remember a conversation with Stewart when he advised me to think about the successful people we knew and how brutally honest they were with themselves about their own strengths and weaknesses. And then he asked me how I could apply this observation to myself. ~Caroline

In addition to developing a business model and understanding opportunities in the market, a manager must also understand the dynamics of an effective leader. Caroline asked herself these questions:

✓ What are the positive attributes of a good leader, and do I possess them?

✓ What are my strengths and weaknesses?

✓ What do I need to improve as I go forward?

Her lifetime of watching teams, analyzing why they worked or why they didn't, allowed her to assess her leadership skills. At This End Up, why didn't we blow apart while going from a handful of stores to over 200, from a regional focus to a national presence? In large measure the success resulted from Stewart's ability to create and lead teams of contrasting players. Caroline considered his methods as she consolidated her lessons on how to lead a team as its president.

Self-awareness is a critical characteristic of successful team leaders.

Studying furniture retail, Caroline knew that the experience she had in each store was due in large part to how senior management had set up the expectations and the working environment. The leadership of a company impacts the associates who impact the customer, and that impacts the profit. She expressed these thoughts at the Furniture/Today Leadership Conference:

Many people feel that if they paint the picture with marketing and advertising, obtain the product, design the stores, even hire the appropriate profile of person, then they will create the identity they seek. We believe that all of those elements are critically important, but it must be bred within organically to resonate. When merely painted on the façade, the identity will stress and crack in the face of challenges.

The secret to weaving it all together lies in the attitudes and beliefs of the senior management team and the process they employ in bringing the brand to life. When the management team creates and articulates the vision, the brand persona begins to radiate out through the departments and the staff until it finally touches the customers through the salespeople and service personnel. ~Caroline

Evaluate the Opportunities

With a working hypothesis in place and a business model identified, Caroline had determined through self-study that she was ready to lead a company. But who was going to finance this company? She approached several manufacturers, including The Rowe Companies, to garner interest in a new retail company featuring specialty upholstery. Having just bought a company called Storehouse and still disappointed in its performance, Rowe had no appetite for another retail company.

Soon after Caroline's visit, Rowe's problems with this new Storehouse purchase reached a critical stage. The leaders were bailing out. Rowe needed a president for Storehouse and they turned to Caroline. In addition to her vision of a new business, she brought valuable experience in the furniture world. She had built a sales team, opened new stores, new districts and a new region, updated the design and merchandise for the stores, had created a successful catalog program, and brought in research and public relations that positioned the This End Up product as a uniquely sophisticated casual lifestyle furniture brand. If she could successfully market This End Up crate-style furniture, what magic could she do with the designs that Storehouse offered?

Storehouse was languishing in lackluster store appearance, disappointing profits, stagnant sales, a distracted management team, and associates who were discouraged and dispirited. These ingredients just happen to be the focus of the Culture of Caring and Caroline viewed the company as an opportunity to fulfill her business model. Could the Culture of Caring bring together profit and people in a company unaccustomed to growth through the relationships between managers, associates, and customers? It presented a transformational opportunity. The senior management team had no experience in developing a people- profit-centered culture, so she was assuming this turn-around responsibility alone.

On the plus side, Storehouse had the number of stores she had envisioned in her model, had a reputation as a lifestyle leader, and a core of dedicated people. She saw the possibility of creating multi-channel transactions, revitalizing product selection, and transforming the sales focus. So, she accepted the challenge. But all those positives didn't eliminate the alarm she felt when she first combed through the financial picture of Storehouse and realized that she faced a long steep climb. Transformation in a difficult environment is tougher than building from the ground up, and this was definitely a difficult environment.

The lesson is to do your research and analysis, make a decision, then go for it. At that point it is either move forward or step aside. And I wasn't stepping aside. ~Caroline

The background story of Storehouse as Caroline entered the scene:

Robert Curry, a highly creative entrepreneur, founded Storehouse in 1969 in Atlanta, Georgia. One of the new lifestyle home furnishings concepts growing around the country, it joined names like Door Store, Workbench, and Design Research. Most are gone now, but the genre inspired the next wave of lifestyle stores, such as Crate and Barrel and Pottery Barn. After he left Storehouse, Robert Curry went on to found a successful lighting business. Storehouse grew to a chain of 40 stores over the next 25 years. The store footprint ranged from about 6,000 to 15,000 square feet. Locations tended to be in specialty shopping areas, with a few stores located in dominant regional malls. Storehouse offered a standard mix of upholstery and case goods with a few accessories. Known as a resource for home office and bookcases, Storehouse helped to furnish home offices and living, dining, and bedrooms in contemporary homes.

Storehouse sales associates were justifiably proud of their internationally sourced and innovative products. In the seventies and eighties, Storehouse was an important regional player in offering products featuring the clean lines of a modern design. It had a captive customer group. If customers wanted contemporary design, Storehouse was often the only store in town. They were among the first to bring important globally sourced products to America. Working with such design-forward products made the sales staff feel cool, and it was cool to be cool. Thus they focused on the product and they measured customers by their perceived taste level.

In the nineties Crate and Barrel and Pottery Barn, both regional players in the home furnishings market, began to use their multi-channel concept, including Internet and catalog, to develop a national presence. As these national brands invaded their geography, Storehouse was unprepared for the new competition and the leaders began to explore an exit strategy. As they were preparing for the sale, Storehouse began to fall behind its competitors, leading to tired and lackluster results. Without leadership, the sales team continued to rely on product uniqueness to generate sales while customers had discovered other venues for contemporary design.

The potential of Storehouse's 40 retail locations attracted the attention of an upholstery manufacturing company, The Rowe Companies. Rowe had already recognized the advantages of vertical integration and established Home Elements, a retail company, to market their own brand of upholstery. Opening new furniture stores is a slow process, and the purchase of Storehouse would speed their progress in the retail segment. Forty stores meant increased demand for their manufacturing plants. The sale was consummated in 1999, and within the next year the entire Storehouse management team left.

A critical factor in Caroline's decision to agree to lead this challenging transformation was the evidence of support for her business model and management philosophy from Rowe's CEO. Through our experience we knew that building a participative culture depends upon having support at the highest decision-making level. She realized that she would be required to maintain her CEO's support through constant communication and early evidence of results.

Perhaps other situations do not seem quite so underwater, but the Pathway to Profit gives value because it works with big problems and small problems. After aligning strengths and weaknesses with the hypothesis and business model, a leader must garner support from the manager, whether that manager is the department head, business owner, or the board of directors. Well-managed expectations will lubricate the gears of a working relationship.

This process will work for leaders in industries other than retail. Imagine the principal of an elementary school. What is the self-interest for making changes? What are the research sources? Who is the customer? What is the business model? How are personal leadership skills determined? How is support garnered from the superintendent of schools? From this process opportunities will emerge.

Once Caroline committed to leading Storehouse, she needed to move forward quickly on the Pathway to Profit, getting the right people in the right place.

Research & Assess
& Define Your Business Opportunity

How do you build your business hypothesis and plan your strategy before you take action?

✓ Identify your customers and determine how you will connect with them.

✓ Determine what's in it for you—enlightened self-interest.

✓ Organize both quantitative and qualitative market research to sharpen your focus.

✓ Develop the model for your opportunities.

✓ Evaluate yourself, your skills and experiences.

✓ Evaluate the opportunities.

Building a team is the challenge

You may be...

- ✓ Hiring an entirely new team

- ✓ Filling vacancies on an existing team

- ✓ Replacing those unable or unwilling to meet expectations

- ✓ Finding the right people for an expanding business

And the question is: Who's going with you?

CHAPTER 2
Who's Going with You?

Before you start a culture shift, selection of your team is critical. Decide who is going with you. People you trust, people with the same values, people who can execute. Look for mindset, intuition, energy, passion, commitment, tenacity, empathy, self-reflection with receptors open, and people who get results through a win-win approach. I value people who are responsive without being reactive, a balance of intelligence and emotional intelligence. ~Caroline

Caroline did not arrive at Storehouse amidst a standing ovation. Although a core group of people remained fiercely loyal to Storehouse, they did not all welcome this new president with her unconventional methods, not trusting her sense of style; after all, she had been selling crate-style furniture—not a sophisticated product. And to them, offering a sophisticated product was their reason for being. They had not requested this change and no one had asked for their input on a new leader. They just wanted to continue as they had been, albeit more profitably.

Managers in all departments had learned to operate the business; they took care of problems and gave instructions to associates. There was no development program teaching managers how to be leaders of their teams and how to develop associates to be future leaders. Job promotions were based on a seniority system and on the willingness of candidates to relocate, rather than a focus on getting the right person in the right place. There was no talent-based selection process.

While they worked together, each department carefully guarded its turf against criticism. Certainly they gathered forces if faced with a common enemy, and they were not too sure whether Caroline was the enemy, or someone to trust to rescue their version of Storehouse. Raise the drawbridge, or lower it to welcome the new leader?

The stakes were high, the deficit was deep, the time period was short, and the people were in the worst throes of uncertainty. Caroline had put herself in the toughest of positions while adhering to her practice of taking a job for what she could learn, rather than what she could earn. Looking back on those first few months at Storehouse, she realized that she had found the hardest job for her skill set, fulfilling one of her personal growth strategies.

If Caroline's new company was to be seen as the best specialty furniture retailer in the market, she would have to lead a change in attitudes at Storehouse.

As she observed her new team she was encouraged to discover the bonds of friendship among associates. It was encouraging that people liked each other. On that premise she would reshape the business.

My immediate job was to build the team, create structure, manage the dynamic of tension between opposing elements, and help the team develop respect and trust of each other's goals. Storehouse would be a challenge to all of the above. ~Caroline

Select Your Managers

Don't count on the people in your company being so compelled by their work that you can energize them, or even retain them, if the leadership at the top is ineffective. There is a trickle-down effect from top leaders that is very difficult to rectify if the flow is negative. Fortunately, the inevitability of the momentum works the same way if the flow is positive. ~Caroline

Changing an organization looms formidable and not for the faint of heart; therefore, leaders will benefit from making it a group effort. Getting the right people in the right place is critical whether starting a new business, leading a company transformation, revamping a department, or improving a nonprofit organization. The most influential team for a company in transition is the executive team, so that is where Caroline started.

Quite frankly, we think a cultural transformation is too difficult to do alone. The "nice to have" is the entire management team leading the change process; the "need to have" is three or four prominently placed fearless opinion leaders. Other leaders need to see the positive results so that they are motivated to become a part of the critical mass.

Alone I could not have shifted the culture fast enough to turn the company around. But with a small group of leaders who shared the vision, we could shift this culture. ~Caroline

In her first few months Caroline focused on her own team. She had vacancies immediately, presenting problems and opportunities. The problem was that part of the organization was without leadership and she was too busy to provide that leadership personally—possible short-term business interruption. The advantage was that she had an opportunity to find leaders who supported her vision—long-term business growth.

She needed a skilled and adversity-resistant team to move this vision on multiple levels. As she defined her thoughts about assembling her team, she followed our guidelines for hiring—determine the job, then the characteristics, talent, and experience that is required to be successful in the job—before selecting the applicant to fill it.

Getting the right people in the right place is critical to the success of your transformation, but oddly enough it is not wise to build your structure around your people. Set the structure of your company around your goals, and determine how the people support the structure, rather than allowing the structure to be set around the people. Counter-intuitively, you will most benefit the people's growth and development by this discipline.

At the executive level I look for good problem-solving and decision-making skills. For insight into the applicant's character, judgment, and process, I explore their thoughts and actions while undertaking major changes. Examining this part of their background gives you insight into how they think. Ralph Waldo Emerson, American poet, lecturer, and essayist, said, "Not in his goals but in his transitions is man great."

I needed the best in the industry in every role. Because of the challenges we faced, I was looking for brave people, people who had been through crisis, people whose character held up through difficult times, and whose individual skills were in focus with the company model I envisioned. Since my plan required collaboration, I looked for people who could be team players. I looked for people I could trust because I needed to give enough room for the senior team to bring their expertise to their craft. Be very careful in hiring people just because you know them. List all your requirements and if the people you know fill those requirements, it works and can save you precious time. But, if they don't have the experience, talent, or temperament they will not succeed and neither will you. And you will have strained a good relationship.

When your skills match the responsibilities of the job, it is possible to soar. To be fulfilled at work people must find opportunities to match skills and jobs. If you are not happy at work, chances are that you are not in the right job. This truth is the same for me as for the people I sought to join the team. ~Caroline

When she first shared this wisdom with Storehouse managers, they were certain that she was telling all of them to leave. No leader had ever voiced the possibility of being happy at work. And if they had ever been told that they should find a job where they could be happy, it was certainly in the "like it or get out" tone of voice. They could not understand the concept of enjoying work until they trusted the messenger.

Dixon joined Caroline right away to fill the vacant merchandising position. Chris joined them first as head of training, then as head of stores when that position became available. Hiring two former teammates was a risk because Storehouse associates were convinced that she would fire them all and bring in her cronies from This End Up, stealing their company from them. Dixon and Chris were well established in their positions before she asked me to join them.

Caroline was wise enough to know that she couldn't be Chain-saw Al and wipe out 800 people. After all, she considered an empowered culture to be her ticket to profitability. Forming that empowered culture at Storehouse meant winning the willing cooperation of associates. The Culture of Caring cannot be dictated from above, but must be built organically within the organization. She knew the principles of the culture, but she had always led a critical mass of dedicated people helping her grow the business. In addition to her own courage, she would need the permission and participation of the people who were already there. An empowered environment works when people understand the responsibilities and advantages of driving results by their own participation, the combination of individual initiative and company focus.

The challenge was to preserve what was good at Storehouse, and there was an abundance of treasure there, at the same time attacking whatever was causing the financial strain and preventing profitability.

While Caroline had positions to fill, she also had members of the senior management staff who had indicated their intention to remain at Storehouse. Her first priority was to get to know the existing team and their responsibilities, assess their skills and willingness to lead the changes, and identify any gaps in the leadership resources necessary to accomplish the vision.

Individual meetings
The success of any management team involves more than job descriptions. Caroline was new to the leadership role at Storehouse and preparing to embark on a culture change, so she created ways to get to know the visions of people who reported directly to her. Individual meetings with each member of the team offered several advantages:

- ✓ To let them know that they were important to the growth of the company

- ✓ To assure them that their leader wanted to know their opinions on the best direction for the company

- ✓ To discover how they proposed that their departments participate

- ✓ To understand what made them feel satisfaction in their roles

- ✓ To see the company from their composite viewpoint, gauging how unified they were in their vision of the company, and the changes they would make

- ✓ To determine how they viewed their own accountability

- ✓ To signal the beginning of the inclusiveness that would change the entire workforce

- ✓ To understand their strengths and opportunities for growth

She didn't underestimate how the choice of questions served to alert the team that there would be changes, while it gave them insight as to what was important.

We found that leaders increased their ability to listen and observe when they gave every person on the team a list of questions to consider before the meeting. It also allowed a comparison of their comments to their actions as we "managed by walking around."

Suggested questions.

- ✓ What do you think we do particularly well as a company?

- ✓ What has been your part in creating this strength?

- ✓ What change would make our strength even better?

- ✓ What would that change look like?

- ✓ How would the change affect the people you manage?

- ✓ Who on your team would have the hardest time adjusting to the change?

- ✓ How would you manage that?

- ✓ What do you see as the 3 top issues that need to be addressed in our company?

- ✓ For each issue, describe the solutions you see.

- ✓ Describe how your team would be involved in the solutions.

✓ Describe our company's culture as it would be if it were the perfect environment for you to be productive and happy at work.

✓ What do you already do to create that environment every day for others in the company?

✓ What is the biggest stumbling block for us in achieving the culture you want?

In sessions such as this, we found that taking notes helped us remember who said what, affirmed the importance of the meeting, and indicated that we were going to use the information given. Questionnaires can be destructive unless action is taken on the information received. A big challenge for Caroline, as it is for most of us, was to resist the temptation to talk too much about her own hypothesis. The purpose of these exercises is to gather information.

As important as gathering information is the analysis of the discoveries. After the meetings, these are some questions Caroline needed to consider:

✓ Do the aspirations of the team match the direction I envision for the company or department?

✓ Do my observations of their interactions with their teams and others in the company confirm the dialogue I had with each manager?

✓ How do the dialogue and my observations mesh with what I hear from people who work directly with the management team?

✓ Do these individuals have the talent and commitment to achieve the changes that will need to be made?

✓ Do they have the support of people they manage?

✓ Do they have a passion for the company's success?

✓ What are the gaps between intention and reality?

In some ways the energy shift may be simpler than it seems. Caroline found that just the act of including her team in determining the future direction of the company began to turn negative energy into positive energy.

In this meeting and analysis format, a new leader may discover that someone on the team doesn't want to play in the new game, isn't completely frank, or doesn't have the ability to play. The cultural change will be easier with 100% of the management team devoted to

"Corporate culture is the most important driver of what happens in organizations, and senior leaders are the most important driver of their organization's corporate culture."

S. Chris Edmonds, SmartBlog on Leadership, March 23, 2012

re-energizing the company, fully equipped with talent and skills to make it happen.

> *To create a positive culture, the leaders must have a strong knowledge of the company's values and the intention to influence the organization. Install energy givers, not energy zappers, on your executive team. This group is the hub that provides guidance and energy to propel you forward. Our job is to give out energy to our teams to fuel the momentum and achieve the goals. ~Caroline*

Having compiled a picture of her team and their readiness for the challenges ahead, Caroline had to determine the strengths and pitfalls facing her. Analysis requires objectivity, with a dash of understanding the vantage point of each person being evaluated. Although it may be tempting to use one of the team members as a sounding board, this practice could backfire. Evaluating and selecting a team are both examples of the saying, "It is lonely at the top." A sounding board, perhaps the head of the human resources department or an outside mentor, could give objective feedback. Concerns must remain confidential until shared appropriately.

Caroline's model for determining her team:

THE KEY TO HIRING

JOB REQUIREMENTS
RESPONSIBILITIES
CHARACTERISTICS

WHAT IS THE
MATCH?
WHAT ARE THE
DIFFERENCES?

SKILLS
TALENTS
EXPERIENCE

WHAT IS NEEDED TO CLOSE THE GAP?
WHAT IS THE COST TO THE COMPANY?

FIGURE # 2 A SYSTEM FOR SELECTION IS A NECESSITY FOR GETTING THE RIGHT PERSON IN THE RIGHT PLACE.

> *I was always mindful that money was flowing through the gap.*
> *~Caroline*

Managers' retreat

In addition to the comprehensive questions in their individual meetings, Caroline scheduled a group meeting to generate sales and profit ideas, giving her another opportunity to assess the abilities and intentions of her team. In sharing their ideas for spurring the business forward, they were building ownership in the program that would become theirs as well as hers.

The first planning meeting with her team was three days. Day one was gathering sales and profit ideas. Day two was a communication session for understanding ourselves and each other. Day three was a decision day. This simple initial three-day meeting structure states more clearly than rhetoric that the company direction and the means to achieve results rest firmly with the team. Because she was assessing her team during this retreat, she invited me (an outside consultant at the time) to lead a communication day, allowing her to observe how the individual members reacted to each other, and give her team a chance to understand her communication preferences. Having an outside facilitator gave Caroline the sounding board she needed to assess her team. If that seems excessive, let's hear from her as to why it was valuable.

> *During our first planning meeting I was amazed at the difference in the quality of the discussion on the third day as compared to the first day. Our stated purpose was to generate sales and cost savings ideas. On the first day participation was pretty disjointed. But after a day spent learning about our own communication preferences as a group and how we could work together, on the third day the ideas came together with more clarity and depth.* ~Caroline

Don't we all work harder when we have set the course?

We refer to this method of decision-making as participative management, the principle being that those who are affected by the decision have a voice at the table, either personally or through a representative. Stewart Brown had shown us that our company would grow stronger and faster by getting the willing cooperation of associates to achieve the desired results. Although Caroline was very familiar with managing through participation, a manager new to this process might benefit from a facilitator who has experience, working closely together to plan the session. An outside facilitator helps curtail topsdown management. Instead of directing the session from the white-board, we found that the team speaks more openly, and more ideas are vocalized, if the manager sits as part of the group. This in no way means that the manager is not managing. In a successful participative decision-making session, managers will ask questions and give perspective, but the team will feel that they were heard and decisions made are theirs.

> **It was an environment [Culture of Caring] that truly believed that we all had something of value to contribute in achieving a common goal, regardless of title or position. The honest communication led to such a sense of inclusion.**
> **~Barb Simmons, This End Up**

Leaders are earning trust with every action, especially in a new and critical situation. There is no room for slips. A bad day is too costly. Every individual on the team has the opportunity and responsibility to be a contributor.

The key to empowerment and success in the Culture of Caring lies in the participative management process. We believe that satisfaction comes from the ability to impact the working environment and participative management allows that to happen for individuals. The leader of the team, having done previous hypothesis building, can guide and shape the input from the team, so that he or she does not lose control over the direction of the goals, yet receives creative and valuable input from the team. And buy-in.

Select Your Associates

Magic happens when there is a match between the right people and the right jobs. Happiness and success are the result. ~Caroline

Of course the critical nature of having the right person in the right place extends beyond the executive team. Having the right executive leaders involved in the process enhances the chances of selecting the right people for every position in the company, if they know how to recognize and select talented members for their own teams.

Storehouse suffered the same malady as other retailers—high turnover at the associate level. Assessing skills and willingness was just as important in other positions as in the executive team, but the immediate concern was hiring people to manage stores, associates to keep them open, and drivers to deliver to customers. When Caroline arrived at Storehouse there was no interview process based on skills and abilities, no succession plan. One of Chris's first actions as vice president of stores was to create a skill and talent based selection and succession plan.

The selection process in the stores was at odds with our belief that the criteria for promotion should be getting results in sales, customer service, individual growth, and teamwork. ~Chris

Years later I answered a question posed on LinkedIn: "Is there a magic formula for hiring . . .?" I responded, "Yes," but like most magic, the feat of hiring the right managers and associates is reality with a twist. Fortunately we were able to teach our managers to do the twist.

Selection Process

The route to an empowered culture lies in ensuring that the right people are in the right roles, and that these roles are structured around the goals of the company. We believe in hiring ability and training skill. Thus, we attracted employees, helped them set goals, and unleashed their energy, then provided training and development to close skill gaps.

We started with initiating an interview and selection process so that every applicant for a like position was evaluated in the same way. The preparatory work may seem extensive, but that work formed the foundation for all interviews. Managers expended great effort in the beginning, but were able to use their foundation with every applicant, thus freeing their brainpower for the evaluation process. No more restricting a search to candidates who had performed exactly the same job in another company. No more just sitting down to chat and hoping that a brilliant revelation would descend. No more depending on the human resources department to make the hiring decision. Managers were making informed decisions.

We believe that a good interview process practiced by an effective interviewer is a better predictor of the applicant's success than standardized tests. It is easier for applicants to represent themselves inaccurately on a standardized test than in dialog with a good interviewer.

Before making a good choice for a position, we have to know:

✓ What is required of the position to meet the company goals

✓ What the person in the position does

✓ What skills, experience, and personal talents are needed to succeed in the position

Just as described for the executive team, we started our hiring process with a comprehensive job description. We could have assigned managers to write job descriptions for each position in the department, but we arrived at a better outcome when the basic job duties were compiled by the person actually doing the work. Who knows a job better than the person doing it? Including associates in creating job descriptions not only gave a more accurate picture of how the associates viewed their positions, it was another example of the inclusion that was critical to developing this culture.

Responsibility by responsibility, task by task, we determined what talent, skill, and temperament helped a person to perform successfully. Selecting the most important characteristics on the list gave a good description of the person to hire. Setting the structure and reinforcing the process indicated who could be successful in which roles.

Once the managers had determined the skills and characteristics necessary for each job, the next step was to create questions to help the interviewer evaluate the applicant by looking for skills, attitude, talent, and experience. We taught every manager how to interview so that every interview followed the same structure. By focusing on the characteristics identified as important to the job, and carefully constructing the phrasing and sequence of the questions, we were able to determine if the applicant had the talent to succeed in the position. Knowing the culture of the organization allowed the manager to determine if the skills and experience would be successful in the environment. For example, a person who works best with structure may flounder in an unstructured free-flowing department.

Every question has a purpose because time is short and selection is critical to success. I recommend blocks of questions to determine each talent, skill, or characteristic. The questions in that block include:

1. A request for a situation illustrating the desired characteristic

2. The role the applicant played in that situation

3. The outcome

4. What the applicant learned to improve performance

This block of questions tells us:

1. What the applicant sees as important. Did the situation described relate to the magnitude and scope of the responsibility in our organization?

2. How important he/she was to the process. Did the role played by the applicant mirror the role expected in our organization?

3. How successful the applicant was. Did the described situation bring the results we are expecting in our organization?

4. How willing the applicant is to learn from experiences. The success of the described situation may not be as important as the applicant's understanding of how to improve performance. We were wary if the applicant did not recognize opportunities for improvement.

The wild card in every interview is the applicant's answers. With a structured interview we are free to concentrate on the answers because the process is familiar.

This method results in a very thorough interview, one that leaves the applicant confident that the interviewer knows as much information as possible to make a good decision. I am not saying that these are easy interviews, but they are effective, indicated by these comments:

> **Just wanted to share yesterday's 'Mantra' that kept me calm for an interview. 'You know you can do this, you passed two Anita Pugh interviews!!' Now I can interview with anyone! ~Michael D. Young, Storehouse**

> **Anita, I must tell you that to this very day . . . I often tell the story of the interviews I had . . . back in early 1997. The interview with you is vivid in my mind as I still recall what we talked about during lunch that day (which of course was your test). . . . It was the most unorthodox day of interviews I have ever experienced. . . . Although I had no intention of taking the job when I arrived, I traveled back home convinced this was the place for me! ~Fabio D. Ruberto, This End Up**

> *A well-planned interview process communicates to the applicant the importance the company places on the position. The interview is often the applicant's first glimpse of your culture. ~Chris*

> *The sound selection process will show your team that each individual is important. This builds esteem and confidence in the team members. ~Caroline*

By structuring the interview to meet the requirements of the position, we hired to meet the goals of our department and company and were not swayed by a gut feeling that we liked, or didn't like, the applicant. Gut feelings are fine, but must be supported by facts in order to build a strong team.

Bill, one of our most successful salespeople, exemplified the wisdom of hiring ability and training skill.

> **I started . . . when I was 22 and just out of college. After 4 months I had no sales but had uncovered lots of leads and prospects, all through cold calls. Instead of being worried about the lack of short-term results, I was given a lot of encouragement. After a few more months, it really began to click. It was surprising how open everyone was to my ideas and new ways of doing things. The most valuable thing I learned about myself was that I could really excel in a non-structured environment, so different from school and anything I had been exposed to. I'm now entering my 24th year in the contract furniture industry and while**

I've never totaled it, I've sold over $65 million in furniture and have trained many salespeople who have successful careers. It was all made possible by a company looking at long-term potential and giving me a chance. ~Bill Levine, This End Up

I distinctly remember my interview with Bill. Although he had absolutely no experience in the area of furniture sales that I was seeking, he impressed me greatly when I asked him why, with his complete lack of experience, I should hire him. Without hesitation he looked right in my eyes and said, "Because I'm not afraid to take no for an answer!" To this day I consider my decision to hire Bill one of the best hiring decisions I ever made. ~Dixon

We set up a system of interviews so that the manager of a position made the ultimate hiring decision, but the next level of management (the "boss") also interviewed the final candidates and gave input and guidance on the hiring decision. This system created at least two interviews for every candidate, and some managers also asked a peer to interview and give feedback. The requirement of multiple interviews did not reflect the interviewer's skill, or lack of skill. A vacant position can put a severe strain on the remaining associates and the manager may face the stress of long hours until the new person is hired and trained. After some time running a short-staffed department, almost any applicant begins to look good. Another manager can see the applicants from a more objective viewpoint and give good feedback. We believe that there should be no surprises once the hire is made.

Many of our suggestions give double value. Involving other managers in the interviewing and evaluation process reinforces the skill of analysis in all the interviewing managers. This sharing of the process strengthens the culture and values.

Sometimes the next level manager (the "boss") found it hard to resist the temptation to override the hiring manager's decision. After all, the boss's own results also depended on the quality of the hire. When the two did not agree on a candidate, the issue didn't reside with the applicant. The issue was the gap in how the interviewing managers evaluated the candidate. The boss's role became coaching the hiring manager to analyze the match between the applicant's responses and the talent needed for the available position.

I know companies that have the human resources department select new associates. Although I led a human resources department, interviewed a huge number of people, and developed some skill in evaluating applicants, I recommend that direct managers make the final hiring decision. Those managers will work most closely with the associates; they will assimilate new associates with the rest of the team; and their results are directly affected by the actions of the new associates. By selecting their own team members, managers are invested in the new hire's success. Setting up the process as described and teaching the managers how to make the selection, organizations can get the right person in the right place by giving managers the decision-making responsibility.

How does this extensive interview process impact those already on the team? Don't discount the fact that there is a certain cachet in already belonging to a team when it is obviously difficult to become a part of the team.

A good interviewer will identify the best candidate for the job and know which areas of concern will need coaching and developing, with a plan in place prior to offering a job. Since the Culture of Caring is based on the development of associates, the early development plan becomes more vital than in other cultures.

Interviews set the tone for future long-term relationships. The process offers applicants a view of our management philosophy. Insightful queries are signals of how our leaders value human capital. Spend the time to discover strengths and weaknesses. Match the strengths to your need and examine your willingness to work with the weaknesses. ~Caroline

I was hired as an 'out of the box' employee, who didn't quite have the full and balanced skill-set needed for the demanding job I stepped into. However, I was told I was hired because in some areas, my experiences and knowledge exceeded those of my fellow colleagues and the fresh insight I brought was viewed as a needed asset to the team. Where my background was deficient, I was given incredible mentoring by an extraordinary group of talented professionals, who honored me with their patience and grace while I negotiated the learning curve. ~Blake Spicer, Storehouse

Succession Planning

We wanted everyone in the company to understand the roles to which they aspired, so that they could prepare to advance through development, productivity, and meeting challenges. A written job description for each position is a motivational tool for skill development and employee growth.

Setting up this interview process not only enabled us to identify the best inside and outside candidates, managers could also use the job requirements as a discussion tool in career guidance.

We partnered the manager and the associate in the associate's development, whether it was skill building for the current position or preparing for a new position. To engage the manager in developing the career path for associates, we gave recognition to the achievement of having someone promoted from a department. Managers who develop new managers are valuable to a company.

A major difference in the Culture of Caring and other environments surfaced when an associate wanted to apply for a job in a different department. At This End Up we set up the first step of the promotion process to be a consultation with the current manager. The hiring manager contacted the current manager for information prior to considering the applicant. Together they decided the strengths and struggles for the different responsibilities and created a plan to maximize strengths and address weaknesses. For this system to work, the associates had to trust that their managers would not block the road.

SmartBrief on Leadership, August 16, 2011, published the results of a poll on handling the movement of talent in a company. Surprisingly only 13% of respondents actively managed the movement of talent through a proactive process. The largest group of respondents admitted to being talent hoarders, making it hard for people to move to new roles. Is it any wonder that talent jumps ship at the first offer from another firm?

Let there be no misunderstanding, creating this uniform system of selecting associates does not mean trying to restrict employees to any particular "type" of person. Although we looked for like-minded vision and values, we recommend diversity of personalities and experiences to strengthen culture. We learn from each other.

> **Caroline embraced our individuality and felt it was important for us to recognize this. ~Debbie Robbins, Storehouse**

We also practiced an analysis when we realized that we had made a hiring mistake because it helped to prevent future mistakes. Consistent analysis fine-tunes hiring instincts. Questions:

✓ What did I see in the interview process that made me think the person could do the job?

✓ What did I miss in the interview?

Hiring the right person for the right job is the manager's responsibility. We believe that hiring managers also bear the responsibility to decide if the job is the right one to benefit the applicant. Unless both the applicant and the company benefit from the employment, there is not a good match. Often the company recovers more easily from a misguided hire than the new employee. Whether the job fails to provide enough challenge, the right growth opportunities, or is beyond the current reach of the applicant, placing the person in the wrong job does the applicant no favor.

> *The whole person comes to work. When personal goals and professional goals are aligned, the result is natural drive and energy leading to success. ~Caroline*

Get the Right People in the Right Place

How do you select members of your team who will be able to produce the desired results for your company?

Select your managers

- ✓ Structure the organization around goals and select the right people to support the structure.

- ✓ Make hiring decisions based on skills and characteristics needed to achieve results in each position.

- ✓ Include diverse personalities, skills and experiences for a stronger team.

- ✓ Have at least three opinion leaders to help you shift the culture.

- ✓ Discover how your managers view the organization, how they manage their responsibilities, and understand their vision for success.

- ✓ Evaluate the gap between intention and reality.

- ✓ Use participative management to promote "ownership" in your organization.

Select your associates

- ✓ Set up a structured interview process to select the most qualified applicant.

- ✓ Educate and empower the hiring manager to make the decision.

- ✓ Develop a succession plan for your organization.

Breathing life into the vision is the challenge

You may be . . .

✓ Determining the purpose of your company

✓ Uniting a team through the vision

✓ Making decisions based on mission, vision, and values

And the question is: Where are you going?

CHAPTER 3
Where Are You Going?

You know that you are ready to determine the mission, vision, and values of your company when you come to understand the current state of your organization and have selected a critical mass of like-minded executives, aligned with visions and values. ~Caroline

The difficulty in getting where we want to be increases dramatically if we don't know where we want to go. While that seems an insult to our intelligence, when asked to describe where the company is headed, associates in many companies may respond with blank stares. It's not that they don't want to know, but more likely that no one has thought to share that information.

In this chapter we are going to talk about missions, visions, and values.

✓ Mission – The ideal of your company, what you want to accomplish

✓ Vision – The path to the ideal, to achieve your mission

✓ Values – The standards and behavioral norms that are important to success in your corporate environment

Establish Your Destination

In some companies the owner or president determines the mission, vision, and values. Other companies determine these by sequestering the top management team until they hammer out statements. We were a part of that second process at This End Up, and it worked well because our culture was already firmly in place. We were simply trying to identify the strengths that existed, so that we could recognize them in new applicants, train and develop them in existing associates, and perpetuate the culture as we grew the company.

At Storehouse we faced a very different situation. There we had a president with a vision, an executive team that was beginning to understand her, but without a stated mission and vision, without a set of unifying values, not everyone felt "ownership" for the company. We discovered visible signs of disengagement, the most blatant being theft.

Then we saw the ultimate sign of a culture adrift—embezzlement. Theft is the physical manifestation of a lack of engagement. Disinterested people take time and they take money. This End Up had provided a great arena for observing people's nature, and we had relentlessly searched for the connection between actions and results. We found that when there was a theft issue, there was usually a lack of connection and a feeling of alienation. ~Caroline

While Caroline labored to align the Storehouse team, Rowe studied the expense of running two retail operations, their original Home Elements and Storehouse. Caroline was a part of the executive team that met to look at cost savings and profit improvement, and from that group came the idea to merge the two retail companies. After a series of meetings on cost control the board determined that the merger improved the profit picture. Besides providing better negotiating power in purchasing and greater visibility for the store brand, they realized that they could cut payroll by combining back office staffing. It seemed a surefire win for stockholders.

The Rowe Companies' decision to combine its two retail operations made the whole culture transition more difficult in many ways, but easier in other ways. Caroline was tasked with merging the two companies, and because Storehouse had more stores and better market recognition, the merged company would be called Storehouse. Almost overnight Storehouse grew from forty stores to sixty, with the inherent problems of different operations, computer systems, delivery operations, products, customer service, and managers.

People don't like change. And now, instead of having one company to lead through the cultural/financial transformation, Caroline had two. Without fast action, fear of the unknown could paralyze the new company. She pulled together the team assigned to work on consolidation. I'm sure they thought the first item on the agenda would be one of the organizational problems. Instead, Caroline asked them to list 3 things that they admired about everyone in the room, about 15 people. These lists were compiled and given to each person. The self-esteem and self-confidence brought about by these positive words allayed fears and paved the way for collaboration.

Acting on their willingness to collaborate, Caroline led them in the process we now call a Pathway to Profit. At the time it was probably more like a pile of paving stones. Ideas, ideals, goals, visions, training and development, coaching, accountability, responsibility, all woven into a loosely constructed plan. The plan became real as we laid the stones.

Establishing the Mission, Vision, and Values

Emotional and intellectual ownership comes from participation. Excellent performance comes from that sense of ownership. ~Caroline

We were determined to give all managers and associates an opportunity to be a part of Storehouse's redirection; and we found a powerful way to involve them. We gave every person in the company the same assignment: Describe the ideal company where you would like to work. They met in small groups and captured the ideas on flipcharts, sending pages and pages of ideas and ideals back to us. This exercise was the beginning of modeling the empowering behavior of open and honest communication. Noting every idea was important for only then would people openly contribute ideas to the group. The end goal was to build the mission statement, vision statement, and values of Storehouse; and the method was to give ownership to every member of the team.

Using pages we gathered from our groups, I arranged ideas into like concepts and noted good descriptive words, such as "customer-friendly," that seemed to incorporate the major concepts. The ideas we gathered fell nicely into about fifteen topics.

When the mass of ideas was condensed to a manageable list of topics, our top management team acted as editor because this process ultimately created the direction of the company. The mission, vision, and values must be important in the eyes of the executive team so that they are in unison on the direction of the organization.

In order to include as many ideas as possible, our first attempts at articulating our mission and vision became a little wordy and required painful editing. Mission and vision statements must be short and concise enough so that associates will remember them. The elevator speech. We have included our Storehouse Mission, Vision, and Value statements at the end of this chapter.

Could Caroline have come up with a mission and vision to give the company the same direction? Of course she could. But, then it would have been hers, not theirs. The resulting words could be exactly the same, but the ownership would be vastly different.

We knew our culture shift was underway when we asked multiple people from different departments to describe the company and they gave us a similar response. Not necessarily word for word, but similar.

Belief in the power of people is charismatic.

100% of the energy of the staff around their ideas is 1,000 times more powerful than 50% of their energy around your ideas. When you are result-oriented it doesn't matter who came up with the idea, it's what's accomplished that is more important. ~Caroline

Were we gambling when we sought to formulate the mission, vision, and values from information submitted by everyone in the company? Could we trust them to give appropriate ideas? The people at Storehouse may not have been able to describe a culture of caring, they certainly did not know how to establish such a culture, but everyone wanted to work in an environment where contributions are appreciated, ideas are considered, and professional development is expected. We knew that we would find success principles that mirrored ours. We focused on the positive impact it would make when we presented ideals they had given, rather than passing down our own divine wisdom. Our trust was well placed. Every idea for our company's direction appeared somewhere on the pages of information we received.

What we learned: You will have lots of opportunities to evoke your wisdom, so use theirs when you can.

Many ideas generated by our exercise with the associates found their way into value statements. Because these values came from the voices of the people, they formed a powerful unifying force.

Values guide associates to make decisions in keeping with the mission and vision of the company and describe expected behavior. Values will vary from organization to organization. For example, our Storehouse associates prized fun enough to make it a value. Fun in a business meant not taking ourselves so seriously as individuals, even while we were taking our dedication to our mission very seriously. In other words, a sense of humor often saved the day. Our definition of fun included the feeling of satisfaction for achievement. Caroline, Dixon, Chris, and I believe that success is fun. Associates are more likely to follow the values when they have a role in establishing them. It is a powerful force.

> I was working for a company that wanted to grow with their people. Leadership was in some ways a team effort, therefore making everyone seem a part of the process. We always had fun and acknowledged the importance of having fun even in stressful times. Happy employees love doing their job even if it is difficult and challenging. . . . My self-esteem soars! ~Cathy Pirtle, Storehouse

Sharing the Mission, Vision, and Values

Assimilating the values into the cultural environment doesn't happen by osmosis. At least for me, that was initially hard to understand. I guess I always thought management had to be more subtle, and that it wasn't so necessary to "name it." Living your mission, vision, and values will not happen without role modeling, but role modeling alone will not make it happen. ~Dixon

To give importance to the role of the mission, vision, and values we chose to present them at the annual business meeting, recognizing that the final product was the culmination of the ideas and ideals gathered from the whole company. After the presentation we held breakout sessions where we coached the managers in communicating the message to their teams. Every associate received a written copy.

To be effective, mission, vision, and values must be more than wallpaper. We are sharing ideas we know work. We initiated some of these ideas, but many were suggestions from the associates themselves:

- ✓ Display the mission and vision on the first page of your strategic plan.

- ✓ Include the statements on your website or intranet.

- ✓ Discuss a value in every newsletter.

- ✓ Encourage managers to use the words in their conversations.

- ✓ Consider values when developing new hire criteria.

- ✓ Make the statements a part of every new hire package.

- ✓ Discuss the mission, vision, and values with applicants who want to join your company to be sure that their values are a match with yours.

- ✓ Post the mission, vision, and values in every office and workspace.

- ✓ Use the mission, vision, and values as a part of performance reviews.

- ✓ Praise associates for acting according to values.

- ✓ Collect and share success stories that reinforce your values.

- ✓ Start a President's Award given each year to the associate who best represents the values in the workplace.

Establishing a common direction was a unifying force designed to bring together two disparate companies, both in the throes of change and disruption.

Other situations may not be as complicated as we faced at Storehouse, but the process of collectively establishing a direction will align a company to manage through mission, vision, and values.

Mission, vision, and values inspire and guide, but alone they do not assure results. Caroline, a great believer in creating a framework, developed a planning and problem solving process we dubbed "thought, word, action." It was easy to remember and it reminded us that our thoughts needed to be shared and that nothing happened without action. These words became the bridge between the intangibles of the mission and vision and the tangibles of goal setting and results.

> *A personal dream, a department goal or a company mission can become reality if you create an action plan to achieve it.*

1. *Inspiration. Shine the light inside yourself, your department, your organization, and be willing to look at and discover strengths and weaknesses, inspiration and motivation.*

2. *Thought. Weave thoughts around the ideal.*

3. *Word. Articulate the ideal, say the words, name the result. If you can give a physical manifestation, that picture of your thoughts will guide you in the next step of the plan.*

4. *Action. Do something, create momentum, apply energy.*

5. *Evaluation. Analyze results.*

6. *Course correction. Repeat steps 1-5 until you get the results you seek.*

~Caroline

Storehouse Mission, Vision, and Values

Mission

To be the best specialty home furtnishings resource in the marketplace

Vision

By making good design readily accessible, we create personal home furnishings solutions for our customers, based on their lifestyles and their dreams.

Values

Profitability

We maximize sales and control expenses to build a successful company that gives greater value to our parent and sister companies and to our shareholders. Every individual looks for ways to improve processes for better productivity.

Commitment

We define Storehouse through our mission, our vision, our values, and our goals. We find the best people to fill every position· people who share our commitment to our customers, to each other, and to Storehouse. As a company and individually, we all are accountable. We are responsible for recognizing the issues we face, focusing on the optimum results, and being action-oriented in achieving solutions. It is this commitment that creates the integrity of the Storehouse brand.

Teamwork

By working together we all achieve more. We recognize and honor our differences as individuals while supporting and respecting each other as a cohesive team dedicated to providing customers an exceptional experience.

Personal Growth

We offer opportunities for individuals to challenge themselves, to be better today than they were yesterday. We expect each person to assume the responsibility for personal growth, in order to enjoy the sense of achievement that follows. We grow leaders who combine an unrelenting focus on the results of our business, with a personal humility that gives credit to other members of the team for our successes. And we celebrate those successes.

Communication

We create an environment to promote the building of trust by giving and receiving honest communication. We develop the skills, practices, and technology that make it possible for us to communicate in an open, timely, and considerate manner with our teammates, our customers, and our vendors.

Creativity

We encourage creativity in the design of our products, our stores, and our marketing tools. We make certain that we have the knowledge and skills to help our customers create design solutions and to meet their service needs. We empower every associate to be creative and action-oriented in solving problems and in providing an exceptional experience for our customers.

Fun

We remember to have fun, because one of the most important things we can do for our company, our customers, and ourselves is to enjoy the process while we are working hard.

*Align Your Company through
Mission, Vision, Values*

---

*How do you change the culture and
profitability of an organization through
your mission, vision, and values?*

✓ Gather descriptions of the ideal organization from every person in every depart-ment.

✓ Compile these ideas into mission, vision, and value statements.

✓ Craft your mission and vision so that associates can remember and express them.

✓ Choose values that will guide the organization's management practices, service ethic, and decision-making.

✓ Live and teach values, assuring that associates understand their individual im-pact on the culture.

Setting goals to accomplish your mission is the challenge

You may be . . .

- ✓ Evaluating your organizational strengths and weaknesses

- ✓ Building company-wide ownership of goals

- ✓ Creating cross-functional collaboration for goal achievement

- ✓ Measuring performance progress

And the question is: How will you get there?

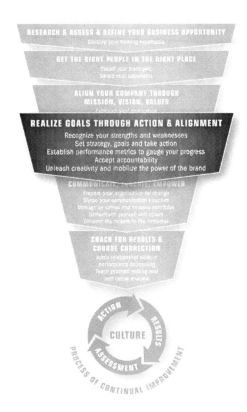

CHAPTER 4
How Will You Get There?

Goals resonate for you personally when their accomplishments tie back to your dreams. When personal goals are aligned with achievement of company goals it unleashes powerful energy and motivation. Then it becomes larger, and you become part of something bigger than you. ~Caroline

Mission, vision, and value statements set the course of a company and describe the working environment. Establishing goals with specific actions, timeframes, and measures gives a basis for anticipating fiscal progress and allows course-correction as needed. In this chapter we address the steps for realizing goals through action and alignment—recognizing strengths and weaknesses, setting goals, establishing measures, and assuming responsibility for results. We use our branding initiative to illustrate the process. Most organizations set goals and we acknowledge that this step in the Pathway to Profit is not atypical, but the process is different.

The Culture of Caring approach is designed to foster collaboration in achieving the desired results, to include all associates in the goal setting and realization process, and to create a sense of ownership throughout the organization. In the Culture of Caring, goals and results become the focus of every member of every team.

As president of Storehouse, Caroline's leadership style was a factor in the process of goal setting and goal realization. Through the synthesis of experience, observing successful people and why they were successful, studying successful principles and why they were successful, she developed these key elements of her approach:

✓ Set the structure to monitor progress.

✓ Maintain balance between the loose/tight control.

✓ Partner rather than boss.

✓ Expect collaboration.

✓ Focus on results.

Recognize Your Strengths and Weaknesses

Before you can create lasting missions, visions, or values, before you can set realistic goals, you must understand your customer, your competition, the sea you are swimming in (your market), and your opportunities and challenges. If you are brave enough to look for and isolate your weaknesses, you will more clearly identify and recognize your strengths. Within your problems are your answers. Learn to see your problems as your source of inspiration, and this will help you to be more willing to address your "brutal reality." Then you set your goals to solve these problems. ~Caroline

This advice does not negate Donald Clifton's premise in the book, *Soar With Your Strengths*. We did identify important strengths in Storehouse that would give us energy to soar and allow the transformation of the profit picture. Over the years the company had leased good locations and established a reputation as a source of contemporary furniture. We enjoyed the backing of our parent company and had some voice in our product selection. The department heads were experts in their areas of responsibility. Many people had developed relationships that were important to them and kept them invested in the company.

Although we agree that we soar with our strengths, we also maintain that it is healthy to identify weaknesses. Actual goals will be different for every company, but the process of determining which problems to solve, the resources required, and the measurements of progress will be similar and must be based on the recognition of the strengths and weaknesses of the company.

When we were well launched on our pathway, we discovered Jim Collins's book, *Good to Great*, which provided a source of inspiration and information for us, and we used it as a mirror to view our progress. I filled my copy with highlighted phrases, some of which reflected my own opinions and others were new thoughts to consider. We found encouragement in seeing that we were on a course that had led other companies to greatness.

Collins challenged us with "Confront the most brutal facts of your current reality, whatever they might be." So that we would not be too discouraged at the prospect of a turnaround company, I also highlighted "Retain faith that you will prevail in the end regardless of the difficulties." With these two thoughts in mind we evaluated our position. Lack of acknowledgment of the brutal realities does not mean that they do not exist.

> *There is strength in admitting weakness. When you recognize a weakness you can minimize it and build confidence. This is the "elephant in the room." Finding the root cause of brutal flaws is digging deep to find the right problem to solve, to find the right thing to work on. Working on the right thing at the right time is a critical success factor. ~Caroline*

One of our brutal realities surfaced in the top management group. Each department had responsibility and accountability for a phase of the business process. When Caroline arrived, the unwritten code of the day appeared to be: Do your job, protect your department when attacked by disgruntled members of another department, and practice the fundamental advice that "a good offense is the best defense." Each department tried to deflect blame to another source if something went awry. The department heads were not accustomed to working together. They saw asking for help as a sign of weakness. Until we addressed our own relationships we would face the same frustrations that caused the company to stagnate in the first place.

We call this separation of departments silo management. Silo management impedes goal achievement in that very few goals are accomplished by one department, having no impact on other departments. This crossover can become the stress point at which companies fall apart, because they have not actively pursued the collaboration that holds the company together. Caroline planned and organized to disallow silo management—departments acting alone. The strength of collaboration and the way she led the team came from inclusion, starting with her and permeating through her team. In discussing goals we recommend that leaders spend time illuminating how goals are shared between departments.

> *The alignment of teams was the opposite of the existing silo management. We began to form a collaborative management process, so that the departments could bring the wisdom of their individual functions to a solution and begin to share the responsibility for the company results. ~Caroline*

In our new alignment every department was responsible for the whole company result. They still had their individual functions, but those functions had to meld together in a process to produce the result, or no one succeeded. Solving issues became a fluid process requiring collaboration and cooperation among departments to achieve the desired results. Changing this thought process proved difficult and took longer than making changes in product or operations. Having Dixon and Chris, two strong opinion leaders, on Caroline's team accelerated the acceptance of collaboration with other departments.

The financial department can be a strong partner in breaking down silo walls because they work cross-functionally with every department, exposing the realities of actual performance compared to goal expectations. I asked Christina Bieniek, the financial guru at Storehouse, what it was like being the one who always had to bring reality to the dreams of every department. She laughed because she knew that I had witnessed her skillful guidance in many a meeting. Her advice:

✓ Keep your finger on the pulse of every area.

✓ Analyze information.

✓ Ask questions.

✓ Pull separate departments together for efficient problem solving.

✓ Offer your help in driving the results.

Christina was not from This End Up. She had not worked in a Culture of Caring environment, yet she quickly realized the value of including the other departments in solving the financial issues Storehouse faced. "And how," I asked her, "did you keep from being the most obnoxious and disliked person on the team?"

Her answer matched exactly what I had observed. "I positioned myself as a partner with every department. I kept abreast of the financial information and was confident of its accuracy. I asked questions to help the department determine where the opportunities were. Then I assured them with 'I can help you.'"

A good example of her help came at a distribution center that experienced rapid growth due to the merger of Storehouse and Home Elements. The head of distribution was "running as fast as he could," but losing ground. The numbers conveyed the brutal reality—our customer service reputation was eroding. Christina partnered with the head of distribution and the head of information technology to reorganize the center and improve systems.

Christina helped to solve a tangible problem—getting our products to customers—at the same time she was tackling an intangible problem—breaking down silo management.

Another example of a tangible weakness was outdated product. Dixon's team immediately began to revitalize our product selection. By updating our merchandise we could impact the look of stores, attracting customers, energizing staff, and giving our brand appeal its first needed boost. This positive change bought us time with our customers, our associates, and our parent company as we worked on intangible issues. Applying the positive energy dynamic from the success of tangible changes encouraged the company's willingness for changes we were yet to make that were not so tangible.

The value of understanding strengths and weaknesses, and then using collaboration to solve issues, does not occur only in the retail industry. I remember speaking with a physician who led a small but critical medical team. She was frustrated that her staff didn't understand the concept of patient focus as she saw it. While she discussed the staff, I realized that they might view her in an ivory tower, the ultimate silo. I believe that finding ways to be more inclusive with her staff would create a team of people focused on the patient. Accessibility is the key to the intellectual and emotional heart of an organization, and our experience has validated that associates who feel included are more committed to the organization's mission.

The process of analyzing strength and acknowledging weakness is the starting point for goal setting. The Culture of Caring is different in that it requires collaboration across all functions.

Effective change is rooted in strong analysis and planning. A strong plan pulls you through the opposition when it feels uncomfortable. When people understand the reason for a change and what it means to them, they are more likely to put energy into accomplishing that change. You will need a well-grounded compass to negotiate through the brutal realities. ~Caroline

Set Strategy, Goals and Take Action

We worked collaboratively to establish our core values, a mission that everyone could buy into (because it was established with lots of work in the field), crystallized our vision, and developed with our teams our strategic plan and our operating plan. ~Caroline

1. Corporate goals

Many organizations set 5-year goals, then 3-year goals with more definition, and an annual operating plan. Long-range goals should support the mission and vision, giving the foundation for each annual operating plan and guiding the proper acquisition and allocation of capital. The annual plan is broken into departmental and individual plans.

At Storehouse the management team established broad categories where we needed to set specific goals.

- ✓ Profitability

- ✓ Operations

- ✓ Brand identity

✓ Product style

✓ Cultural development

✓ Customer experience

Effective goal setting starts with understanding the economic engine of the company and each position's ability to affect it. Inclusiveness comes by developing programs for teaching financial literacy to associates. Then the associates can learn to analyze their performance data and relate it to the company's performance, which enables them to be effective participants in the company goal-setting process.

In keeping with the strength of our resources, we selected four key initiatives from the broad categories; not that we had only four issues we needed to address, but we had to channel our resources for greatest impact.

For example:

1. What is most important for driving sales growth?

2. What is most important for operational improvement to reduce costs?

3. What cultural goal will make the biggest impact on company performance?

4. What is the most important brand/merchandising initiative?

Limiting the number of corporate goals will help associates to be more focused and engaged in the active achievement of each goal. ~Dixon

In the Culture of Caring, goal setting is a bottoms-up/tops-down exercise. Each year department heads asked their teams to submit ideas for the key initiatives—sales growth, cost reduction, culture and brand strengthening. The ideas were culled by the department and submitted to the executive team at a three-day meeting devoted to setting the year's goals and initiatives. Pages and pages of flipcharts lined the walls as ideas were listed and discussed for viability. Bottoms-up. Each department left the meeting with broad goals in each category. These goals were then presented to our middle managers to determine how each one would be achieved and measured. Once the initiatives were formalized, department goals were presented to the associates and everyone set personal goals as their part to play. Tops-down.

Using a "bottoms-up" method, we included all associates in setting company goals. This inclusiveness gave us greater assurance that all associates would own the goals. ~Chris

The Culture of Caring includes everyone in establishing, sharing, and achieving goals.

2. Department goals

When the goals are shared, each department understands the collaboration needed, revealing roadblocks to be removed.

Goals might receive the stamp of approval by the executive team, but achievement was dependent upon departments and individuals. Every department manager introduced the company goals, then set departmental goals to meet the objectives. Departments determined who would be responsible, what departmental and cross-functional resources would be needed, and the time frame for completion.

> **The team atmosphere was always present. It didn't make a difference which department you worked in or location, it was just there. It was an accepted practice within our culture. ~Ann McCormack, Storehouse**

3. Individual goals

With our goal setting process we found that when individuals understand their roles and how they fit into the achievement of the company's goals, they feel like they count. And that "counting" is the foundation for the Culture of Caring. When associates know the company goals and their goals and work hard to meet them, they not only gain satisfaction in meeting their own goals, they are now connected to the whole and the company's success.

> *Seeing that you make a difference is a key component of employee satisfaction. You want to see the company win because you know that you had a part to play in its success. ~Caroline*

Department goals influence individual goals. The manager worked with every individual to formulate goals that impacted department goals. Once again, the individual goals were measurable and had a time frame.

Think of this as a pyramid, much like the cheerleaders create. Individual goals support department goals, which support company goals. This goal-setting method ensures that everyone owns the company goals. When individuals meet their goals, the department meets its goals, and the company meets its goals. If expectations are set high enough, the company is on the Pathway to Profit.

THE GOAL STRUCTURE

FIGURE # 3 THE GOAL STRUCTURE RESTS ON THE FOUNDATION CREATED BY THE VALUES AND SUPPORTS THE MISSION AND VISION.

The Culture of Caring creates ownership of company initiatives.

To make a mission more than a dream, more than wishful thinking, you must create a plan and apply action. Your goals are your guide-posts showing you the way. Your strategy is your action plan to achieve your goals. Successful advances toward your mission require:

✓ *Building the structure to achieve your mission*

✓ *Obtaining and deploying the resources necessary to achieve your goals*

~Caroline

Establish Performance Metrics to Gauge Your Progress

When you manage for results, the process allows people to develop at their own pace and you will see facets of brilliance emerging. ~Caroline

We devised metrics, both financial and behavioral, so that we could see the variance between where we were and where we wanted to be. Reading the financial map became our tool for solving problems. Using analysis to plan our route, coaching and counseling behavior toward performance improvement was our method.

How do we know when we have achieved the result we desired? Besides that feeling of satisfaction derived from something apparently going right, setting goals with measures gives the real identification of achievement. Breaking those goals into performance metrics provides a method to gauge progress toward goal achievement. How much is enough? When have we hit a home run?

On the Pathway to Profit, the financial department moves to front and center in establishing tools to measure performance, defining mileposts to success. Christina and her financial department were our leaders as we developed Key Performance Indicators for each department. These statistics measured individual and team performance. Christina compiled the results disclosed on financial reports, but she also assigned importance to the critical measures that were milestones to these results. At this level we measured the pulse of activity that drove sales and controlled costs. Storehouse had not previously measured Key Performance Indicators.

Examples of the indicators that Christina's team measured for us: The marketing department had sales goals for each event, the merchandising department had sales and margin goals for each product category, and the logistics department had inventory and delivery completion goals. The sales department had performance indicators measuring the number of orders and size of the orders, both in dollars and number of products, and sales compared to traffic. In each of these areas the finance team helped departments break down statistics into individual goals. Thus the pyramid: Individual goals achieved meant department goals achieved, which meant company goals achieved. The financial reporting gave us the information to evaluate our success.

Profitability depends on the whole team, not just the revenue generators. In both our companies we sought to impact the sales revenue through ease of operation, minimal red tape, and efficiency. The support team provided the basis for this foundation on which we built our sales strength. When we developed performance metrics for our behind-the-scenes players, they too were able to judge their progress.

Along with the establishment of the performance metrics we initiated training with every department to develop the financial skills and literacy of the associates so that they could see their part to play in creating those results.

Key Performance Indicators enabled us to uncover problems and practice positive course correction. The numbers only indicate where the problems lie. The head of a department or a company is responsible for the results. Waiting until the initiative fails and throwing blame on someone else is not an option in this culture.

Caroline got in when the "sausage was being made," rather than waiting until the end. She did this through a structure of appropriately timed meetings designed to give her the information she needed to ensure that we were on track. ~Chris

Caroline was well aware that people wanted to feel that they managed their own business and she wanted them to have that sense of ownership. To accomplish this she had to develop a structure, the "sweet spot" between control and freedom. She remembered a stroll down the beach with her college roommate years earlier when her friend asked her to pick up a handful of sand. She realized that as she held it loosely her hand retained the sand, but when she squeezed her fist, the sand escaped.

You have to convince yourself that your action of consciously not reacting actually gives you control of the situation. Hold too tightly on the reins and the horse may trip. Loose reins give the latitude for the horse to make some decisions. ~Dixon

OK for sand and horses, but how to translate this wisdom to maximizing the infrastructure of a struggling company? Managing capable people is similar to that sand exercise. Micromanage and lose their initiative; give independence and they want to work with you.

Caroline's concept of partnering with members of her team and developing their independence gave each of them a model to use with their own teams. By establishing performance measures the managers had their own milestones giving them the independence to arrive at the one version of the truth that is undeniable, the results.

One of the ways she gave her executives control occurred when they came to her for mediation. Although she could have given them the direction they sought, she often sent them back to work it out themselves, knowing that they needed to feel the ownership and only their interaction would reveal the best solution for the company and grow their collaboration skills. This was an early lesson learned from Stewart Brown.

Hierarchy gives you the boss label. Partnering gets the willing cooperation because it gives ownership to the other person. In solving the issues we faced, each department manager had a part to play and the responsibility to work with others to solve the whole. Every day I asked myself, "How do I lubricate the gears that make the team work?" ~Caroline

Our experience showed that selfless leaders win because they don't have to insert themselves in the solution; they manage for results. However, successful leaders determine the critical juncture for course correction to prevent needless unproductive energy expenditure. They balance their controlling urge with a show of trust in people to think through issues and solve problems.

This was not a runaway wagon. Those reins were never really out of my hands. However, my confidence in the quality and talent of the managers, the structure of collaborative goal setting, constant communication, and consistent course correction allowed the team to feel the independence. ~Caroline

Accept Accountability

Although our vision was large and ambitious, we were conscious that too much vision can be daunting, so we broke our plans down into more manageable steps so that each person could understand. We developed confidence in building to the edge. Then we moved the edge. Then we grew. ~Caroline

As we led Storehouse in the Pathway to Profit, our company stumbled more than once. We faced a problem faced by most companies—we did not always meet our goals. We sometimes missed the connection between expectation and execution. Most people believed in the goals—after all, they had helped to establish them—but not everyone felt personally accountable for achieving them. Someone else would pick up the slack. The tendency was to see external issues as reasons for underachieving. Any excuse would do so long as it involved actions that the associate could not control. Fortunately for us, when some locations were down, others were up. We challenged ourselves to heighten the focus on personal accountability so that associates made a connection to actions they could control. We discovered that breeding ownership is challenging because the vision must be simple and clear, at the same time allowing room for a stretch. We introduced accountability through coaching and counseling performance metrics.

[Chris] held me accountable by explaining the magnitude of my impact and being an example to other leaders in the company. ~Christy Carpenter, Storehouse

For performance metrics to impact profitability we had to invite Harry Truman's buck to stop at our place. We needed an attitude adjustment, a balance of interdependence between departments and a willingness to accept responsibility for the actions in our own departments. Accountability starts with the executive team.

As we solved problems we did what we said that we would do; we held ourselves accountable. ~Caroline

We knew that we must stay focused on the result, understanding that the work styles may be different. This was true within the executive team and when leading our own teams. ~Chris

What makes up accountability in the Culture of Caring?

✓ Goals

✓ Measures

✓ Timeframes

✓ Understanding your own role

✓ Coaching

✓ Consequences (both positive and negative)

How is accountability different in the Culture of Caring? Goals, measures, timeframes, and understanding our own roles all contribute to accountability in any organization. In the Culture of Caring we started the recovery process with coaching development, rather than punitive discipline. Consequences do not go away, but are clearly communicated in coaching.

People who joined our company were often accustomed to viewing accountability as punitive rather than an opportunity to develop. The idea of having a development plan to correct a weakness was a new thought for many, and we spent hours teaching our managers to conduct these conversations. ~Chris

Before we could achieve a change in attitude, we had to educate. For example, we put in place monthly coaching sessions in the stores to teach financial literacy along with the relationship between sales results and associate behavior. These monthly sessions brought accountability to the individual on each team.

It was exciting to see people connect the dots between selling behaviors and statistics. The sales team began to see that what they did on the sales floor had an impact on many of their individual statistics. Realizing they had control was very empowering. ~Chris

Identify "controllables"

We knew that our associates came from jobs where they were held account-able for the end result, no matter what the circumstances. This can be counter-productive. With a more positive approach, we helped them to determine what they could control, then set goals high enough so that we were achieving the end result through "controllables."

For example, the ultimate measures of store success are the sales metrics, including volume and same-store sales. We knew that we could increase sales through the development and implementation of our unique selling program. Associates might not be able to control the construction that blocked the street in front of the store, but the customer experience inside the store existed well within their purview to control. With that expectation we could hold them accountable for:

- ✓ Mystery shop reports that measured customer experience

- ✓ Number of transactions vs. store traffic

- ✓ Dollars per transaction

- ✓ Items per transaction

- ✓ Individual coaching for skill development

- ✓ Building a customer connection

Another example: At This End Up our home delivery drivers experienced frustration because they did not see that they could control anything about their experience with the customer. They considered themselves at the mercy of the customer's demands. As director of training and development, Chris helped them to find their "controllables":

- ✓ Their own appearance. Customers reacted more favorably to a professionally attired delivery team.

- ✓ Their conversation. If they began the delivery with a friendly approach, most customers responded in kind.

- ✓ Their own attitude toward service. The customer could sense if the delivery team saw their role as being there to help, or saw the customer as an opponent.

- ✓ Their reactions to the customer. Even with a difficult customer, a positive reaction eased tension.

Identifying "controllables" instilled confidence and self-esteem in the drivers and the aura of confidence and self-esteem translated to more coopera-tive customers and easier deliveries.

Coach

Coaching and development programs define the difference in accountability between most companies and the Culture of Caring. The relationship that results from the honest communication around performance improvement cements the bond between manager and associate. Performance measures uncover roadblocks; coaching and development programs increase skills. We mastered those roadblocks by identifying the most effective activities leading to the end result, then educating and coaching associates to be effective in these activities. If there is a gap in performance it could be a willingness issue, rather than a skill issue. Although willingness issues may appear, they are less likely in this culture. Instead of "It's not my job!" we were more likely to hear, "It's our company." In the Culture of Caring coaching precedes performance consequences.

> *Along with coaching and counseling we documented results so we could celebrate our wins and course correct when we missed. Our goal was to help associates create their own "roadmap" for success. ~Chris*

Although most associates did create their own roadmap for success, some didn't. We found the need to enact punitive consequences was greatly reduced when we helped associates identify "controllables," set our expectations so that mastering "controllables" gave the result we wanted, and developed their skills so that they excelled in the actions they controlled.

Consequences

Lack of skill or lack of willingness does happen, and we prepared our managers to handle the consequences phase, adhering to the same values that guided our business. Associates, including those not directly involved, benefited from the knowledge that the manager would take action when performance problems began. The objective was to improve performance, but if associates must leave, allowing them to leave with dignity affected not only those leaving; it had a ripple effect throughout the team. The team saw that the associate was treated fairly, that the manager was committed to good performance, and that those remaining no longer had to carry the load for those not performing to expectations.

Unleash Creativity and Mobilize the Power of the Brand

> *As a leader you may see it and know it, but your job is to get others to name it and do it. ~Caroline*

Revitalizing our Storehouse brand was one of the most apparent challenges in transforming the profit picture, so we will use brand initiatives as examples of realizing goals through action and alignment. When we could turn our attention to unleashing creativity, we knew that our flywheel was spinning, as Collins described in *Good to Great* and we were excited to be able to think about the art and science of creativity.

> *Learning to look at your difficulties, simply searching for the treasures—that's what sets you up for creativity. Creativity begins with a problem. ~Caroline*

Brand encompasses every aspect of the company-customer relationship—the products or services it sells, the marketing initiatives, its global Internet presence, and the people who represent the company. Storehouse needed to revitalize every area of brand and this is how we did it.

Caroline and Dixon began building the merchandising department by studying the apparent strengths and weaknesses in the existing organization. Dixon inherited a team with recognizable strengths:

1. They were comfortable with the buying process.

2. They knew the market.

3. They followed trends.

4. Their personal taste levels reflected our customers.

5. They had creative ideas.

6. They wanted Storehouse to be the place to go for contemporary furnishings.

The areas of weakness Caroline and Dixon recognized:

1. Silo management within the department

2. Silo attitude toward the rest of the company

3. Lack of focus on the science of merchandising

4. No consumer-focused research process on which to build the brand

5. Ideas emanating primarily from the senior managers

6. Lack of awareness of components of brand and how it all fit together

1. Silo management within the department

Dixon found the merchandising buyers as firmly ensconced in their individual silos as whole departments had been. The buyers were assigned to upholstery, case goods, or accessories and they selected what they liked and thought would sell, with little consideration for the other components. If they needed to set up a photo for advertising, they worried about how it all went together, but otherwise they were accustomed to selecting individually. In order to present a coordinated presentation to the customer, Dixon would have to break down the silos and he needed their willing cooperation to make this change without disrupting business.

Faced with making an intangible change, breaking down silos, Dixon started with a tangible change. He set aside a room in our office that became known as the "war room." Fabrics and accessories were displayed on shelves. The merchandising team covered the walls with pictures of upholstery, case goods, and accessory products they favored, combining the images in coordinated collections. The prospect of putting it all together brought a buzz of excitement for this new creative challenge and the buyers found themselves working together. No more uncoordinated buying. Our store customers, immersed in a visual picture of the completed room design, were more likely to purchase multiple pieces. Once each quarter the buyers met in that room lined with product wallpaper and presented to Caroline their research and analysis by category. More sales potential enabled the department to set more ambitious sales goals. Establishing performance metrics allowed them to track how customers reacted to their collections. The ability to track results gave them accountability. Through this process Dixon introduced them to the science of Storehouse merchandising.

2. Silo attitude toward the rest of the company

The relationship between the merchandising department and the rest of the office improved with the establishment of that war room. Our office space was never quite large enough, so we needed to maximize every square inch. When the marketing and merchandising teams were not using the room, it was open to everyone in the office. Other departments held meetings there, teams brought projects to spread out on the tables, people walked through to get to the other side of the building. It was a good utilization of space and allowed everyone in the office to feel a part of the merchandising process as we viewed product development on the wall. Inclusion of the behind-the-scenes teams—priceless.

The merchandising department viewed themselves as style mavens for Storehouse, but they did not sell the product; that was the role of the sales team. Because the customer ultimately determines the success of products or services, our sales team had always been invited to a merchandising meeting to critique the product selections. Before Chris led the sales team, these meetings had been difficult encounters, with questionable value other than an opportunity for both teams to vent. After his first such meeting, Dixon vowed he would never sit through another. The challenge was to gain feedback in a more collaborative manner.

Those dreaded meetings, where the Storehouse sales people could complain about the products, disappeared and in their place we began gala evenings once a year. We completely re-merchandised one store, introducing new products selected at market. The gala soiree was combined with the already scheduled managers' meetings and became a chic, fun event. While the atmosphere was more like a cocktail party with a theme, the managers wandered the store and used their note cards to write their feedback on new products. Their feedback was more positive and yes, the buyers did use it to impact future merchandising direction.

That may sound like a party, but it was a process of creative collaboration that led to an alignment of the sales, marketing, merchandising, and logistics departments. Rather than a demoralizing critique, the merchandising gala became a rallying point for renewed energy. The party bolstered the sales team's enthusiasm so that they approached their customers with a genuine appreciation for the products they offered.

Dixon's collaboration strategy included more than a war room and a big party. He set up regular meetings with every department to discuss mutual issues in achieving cross-functional goals. The silo walls began to crumble.

3. Lack of focus on the science of merchandising

The art of creativity (the intuitive part of the process) in a collaborative company begins with a common vision and allows room for individuality. With a talented team and an organized system for risk taking, the process gives rise to an energized result. The science of creativity (the analytical roadmap to decision-making) uses research and data analysis as its foundation. A leader gives the art to the scientific players, and the science to the artistic players, weaving together art and science to unleash the creativity of the team. ~Caroline

Merchandising is based on the blend of art and science. Art = trend, talent, and intuition. Science = analysis and research. Although strong in the art, Storehouse buyers had not been coached in the science of merchandising. The challenge was to create a process whereby they could evaluate results through established performance metrics compared to product sales.

As Caroline and Dixon coached the science and art of merchandising they used these questions:

Science

✓ What does your analytical information tell you?

✓ Can you distill the Darwinian theory? (The survival of the fittest, an analysis in which the most successful product survives, the merely healthy product is adapted, and the unsuccessful products become extinct.)

Art

- ✓ Who is the target customer?

- ✓ What does the trend and customer research tell you?

- ✓ What does your inspiration and intuition tell you?

- ✓ What is the product (or service) development direction?

- ✓ How does the aesthetic umbrella inform the process?

Caroline and Dixon pulled the diverse and artistically creative merchandising team together and taught them the science side of the blend by teaching them to be analysts. They reported on their own categories and clarified their own pathway to profit. Dixon conducted pre-market meetings with each buyer to review the market plans and share ideas. They studied the analytical reports, incorporated market research and style trends to set the agenda for their week at the furniture market.

> *Support the creative process. It is like a river that flows in unusual ways from its source (the idea) to the delta (its execution). As the leader your job is to influence upstream, at the beginning of the idea, then to course correct along the way to keep the river in its banks. If you find that you are changing the project when it reaches the end (at the delta) you will need to review your process. You hamper creativity in your organization if you wait until the work has been done to give your input. Your job is to set up the process so that you give input at the beginning and along the way, then unleash the force to get the job done. ~Caroline*

For example, Caroline used the quarterly analysis and trend meetings to affect the merchandising direction and Dixon used his one-on-one meetings and pre-market meetings to inspire and coordinate the buyers.

We made calculated risks and took personal opinions into consideration. We practiced inclusiveness, brought in the ideas of others; but we used the art and science process, not just gut feelings, to achieve our successes. No longer did the loudest voice in the room drive the decision. And we let the customers vote with their wallets.

4. No consumer-focused research process on which to build the brand

Storehouse had never utilized consumer-focused market research. They had established stores, advertised in local newspapers, and waited for the customers. As the flywheel began to turn, we engaged the Yankelovich research team to study our target customer. Knowing which groups of people were likely to purchase our style in our price-range allowed us to spend our marketing dollars wisely, targeting magazines they preferred, sending direct mailings to selected customer lists, and choosing convenient store locations.

A group we called the color team began trend research, weaving color, behavior patterns, arts, fashion, and media to create color themes. Their role was to understand and stimulate consumer behavior.

5. Ideas emanating primarily from the senior managers

Get the "I" out and the "we" in. Learn to get your strokes by seeing others succeed. Learn to make the associates the heroes. This requires an emotional strength to resist drawing the attention to yourself, but turning the attention to others so that they succeed, and therefore you succeed. ~Caroline

Old Chinese Poem:

"Go to the people.

Live among the people

Learn from them.

Start with what they know

Build on what they have.

But of the best leaders,

When their task is accomplished

Their work is done,

The people will say . . .

We have done it ourselves."

Usually making someone else the hero will be easy, but not always. There are times when we want to say, "I thought of it first!" Just don't! Eventually the environment brings creative thinkers and the reward of results.

As the department gained momentum in collaboration, inclusion and ownership, Caroline's watchful eye alerted her when too many ideas seem to come from the executive team. In other companies executive team ideas would be assurance of outstanding performance, but in the Culture of Caring, that strength could indicate lack of development of talents within the teams—short-term success at the expense of long-term growth.

Dixon considered the merchandising department as the "keeper of the creative flame" and he led by example. He sought design ideas from art objects and nature as he traveled to exotic countries in search of products that would enhance the lives of our customers.

His challenge was to create an environment that would evoke a flow of ideas from his entire department. I developed a creativity workshop for marketing and merchandising teams, focusing on releasing their ideas and fostering collaborative development of creative solutions to problems and opportunities. In that safe setting we explored the sublime and the ridiculous as we opened our minds to idea generation. We had such fun that they didn't question why we felt the urgency to bolster the creative process. Often schools and employers have squelched creativity so effectively that associates will not recognize value in every idea. This attitude surfaced as a hesitation to participate, or in the scoffing of someone else's idea. When everyone on the team understood the openness of the creative meeting model we increased green light thinking. We knew that when a team would not let anyone stampede an idea through, nor allow anyone to squelch a teammate's idea, we would unleash creativity.

> *"Our task is not to see what no one else has seen, but to be able to look at what everyone else is seeing, and to think new thoughts about that which everyone sees."*
>
> *Schopenhauer,*
> *German philosopher*

I believe the greatest impact was the lesson to listen, to try to see others' perspectives, to respect others' talents and experiences. Those things were reinforced in both our formal team building and in the everyday work environment. ~Mary Warner Hart, Storehouse

The key is to establish an environment of trust, with open and honest communication on an ongoing basis, when you build a culture of innovation. Ideas must be incubated in an environment that encourages risk. ~Caroline

How do you teach someone to be brave enough to try new things? One example of green light thinking was what we called our "skunkwork" studio. We had five studios where we allowed the buyers to create and take bigger risks. Each studio provided a place for buyers to play, but a very controlled test, so that a study of our results gave us proven products to add to our overall product assortment. The challenge is to find an avenue for the creative process, a project that will not derail the company if it is not successful, but can be duplicated if it is successful.

If Columbus had concentrated on the probability of sailing off the edge of the world instead of the possibility of finding a new trade route to the Indies, would he have ever sailed off toward the western sunset? ~Dixon

Make no mistake. There is no platform for creativity unless the financial and logistical structure is in place to support the creative process. As important as recognition for creativity is the recognition of the behind-the-scenes work that supports the organization. Although we are used to thinking about creative people as just being creative and business people as being, well, business-like, the combination produces a creative businessperson—a treasure for a company.

6. Lack of awareness of the components of the brand

Creative branding was not complete until the customers understood the message; so we built our brand through product selection, store presentation, media, and the associates in the stores. We created a cycle of brand awareness through our presence in national magazines. Caroline's smiling face became the face of Storehouse. People came into the stores and talked about Caroline as if she had personally reached out to them. And she had. The full-page displays showed a sophisticated product with a people-centered presence, setting a tone for the in-store experience. Our role in the stores was to live our brand.

> *Branding elevated the mystique of working with our company. Seeing our full-page color ads in shelter magazines and product recognition in feature articles helped associates to feel important in the field of home furnishings. ~Chris*

Caroline saw accessibility as a necessity in building the Storehouse brand. We defined accessibility in the broadest of terms: product selection, easy access to stores, catalogs, phone orders and Internet, convenient delivery to the customer's home.

We wanted to be the friendly neighborhood store with the price advantage that comes through the buying power of a sixty-store chain. We designed stores with products that gave the customers ideas they could use in their own homes. We grabbed their attention in our people-focused advertising; we promised them that we cared about them; and we assured them that the sales team would give them good design guidance in the realization of their dream rooms. Our goal was to have associates and managers in our stores act like they owned the store. The larger the chain, the more difficult it is to create this brand identity.

> *What does it mean to have the heart and soul of an individual proprietor with the buying power of a national company? I refer to it as a "please touch experience" for the customer. To achieve this feel of a local personalized store rather than an institutionalized national chain, we addressed the store from merchandising, marketing, and the in-store experience. In our merchandising approach we created warm, inviting vignettes to welcome customers. No two stores were alike. We*

allowed for a bit of risk in our merchandising assortment. We switched from product-focused to customer-focused marketing. Our national advertising included pictures of people as well as product. ~Caroline

While the brand message may be aimed at the customer, its benefit is internal as well. Brand and culture are intertwined because the visual cues of brand (product, presentation, media, and customer experience) are reflective of a company's cultural values. Pride of ownership is contagious—peer-to-peer, associate-to-customer.

I always had a vision that our public relations, advertising, and marketing efforts were as important in energizing our internal associates as they were in attracting our external customers. The subtle identity cues that came from the branding effort gave our people an even crisper vision of their part to play in carrying out the brand promise. ~Caroline

"You need to present a coherent and plausible sense of yourself as an organisation. That means having a robust employer brand: knowing who you are, and being able to tell a good story about yourselves. This happy scenario will not come about by chance. It requires leadership and a sustained communications effort. You may need to bring to the surface your organisation's values and attitudes that have remained tacit or undiscussed until now."

Stefan Stern in the Financial Times on August 31, 2009

Examples of companies who practice brand identity:

✓ Nordstrom – not only symbolizes an upscale fashion-driven department store, but is also recognized for its excellent customer service.

✓ Nike – promotes outstanding sportswear and equipment while also standing for a healthy and active lifestyle.

✓ L.L. Bean – offers fine products for outdoor enjoyment and lives its message through encouraging associates to participate in wholesome outdoor activities.

✓ Disney – represents imagination and entertainment through the Magic Kingdom, where a "cast member" sounds more fun than employee.

As you build your own success story, use the power of a well-aligned brand to energize and inform associates. Align the visual cues—sales, marketing, merchandising, space design, visual merchandising, catalog, and web. Then align the support services for maximum impact. This creates visual roadmaps for identity and instills passion and energy in both the customers and the associates. ~Caroline

Dixon and Caroline used every part of the goal realization process as they revitalized the Storehouse brand. The customers met our new creative process when they visited our stores and, through Chris's influence, our stores began to reflect the image we portrayed in our public relations and advertising. Our profits increased as our customers identified with our brand.

Realizing goals through action and alignment in the Culture of Caring involves collaboration between individuals and departments, inclusion of everyone in setting direction, and company-wide ownership for actions and outcomes. Leaders establish the framework for success by creating the structure, guiding the process, and focusing on results.

Realize Goals through Action and Alignment

How do you set goals to support your mission and vision, commit the resources, and establish measures to determine success?

Recognize your strengths and weaknesses

- ✓ Identify your strengths.

- ✓ Face your brutal realities.

Set strategy, goals, and take action

- ✓ Develop a strategic plan for three to five years.

- ✓ Determine which problems to solve, the resources required, and the measurement of progress.

- ✓ Build your annual operating plan so that company goals are supported by department goals and department goals are supported by individual goals.

Establish performance measures to gauge your performance

- ✓ Identify the Key Performance Indicators that support your goal achievement.

- ✓ Educate and coach associates to relate behavior to performance indicators.

Accept accountability

- ✓ Manage accountability on an individual and department level.

- ✓ Coach associates to identify "controllables."

PATHWAY TO PROFIT
PART 2

Creating a Relationship-based Culture Focused on the Customer

"Everyone thinks of changing the world,
but no one thinks of changing himself."

Leo Tolstoy

Preparing people for success
is the challenge

You may be...

- ✓ Building a communication structure

- ✓ Developing leaders

- ✓ Creating learning opportunities

- ✓ Improving customer relations

And the question is:
How do you get everyone on board?

CHAPTER 5
How Do You Get Everyone on Board?

Culture is not just painted on, you have to work organically, internally until it infuses the fiber of every element of the company. Only then does your customer experience the culture. ~Caroline

Part 1 of the Pathway to Profit shows how to build organizational architecture that lays the foundation for profitable growth. Part 2 shows how to include every associate as an integral part of the company mission, vision, and values, creating customer synergy—resulting in increased sales and profitability.

Changing organizational architecture could cause transition trauma, but we anticipate that the most dramatic changes a company experiences will be in the way people impact each other and interact with customers. This stage of the pathway describes education, coaching, and individual growth. We show how to develop the skills, expectations, and knowledge for associates to achieve beyond their recognized abilities. Using principles of the Culture of Caring we discuss leadership, change, communication, conflict management, problem solving, teamwork, and performance counseling—all leading to healthy relationships.

Caroline was so convinced culture was the key to profitability that she established a position dedicated to developing the skills that create success in the new culture. This was a bold move in a company of less than a thousand people. When she first approached me with her plans for the transformation of the Storehouse culture, she offered me a challenging opportunity—to develop leaders who had never worked in a value-based management system, to engage associates who felt powerless to impact results and were leery of the strange ideas being voiced by their new president. Of course I was intrigued. My personal goal was to take what I had learned from Stewart Brown at This End

Up and use it to impact the profits of another company, making Caroline's offer just the opportunity I was seeking. That said, although I understood exactly what she intended to accomplish and I had a good picture of the culture we were creating, I admit to being a bit overwhelmed as to how to start. A picture always helps me to develop the process of getting there.

Like our early ancestors I created a wheel, and once I had it on paper it became clear how to accomplish Caroline's vision. Trust me, the wheel in this chapter is a much improved version of my original circles and spokes, but the picture sparked the plan.

FIGURE # 4 THE WHEEL REPRESENTS HOW WE TRANSFER THE IDEALS OF THE COMPANY TO CUSTOMERS. THE SPOKES (MANAGERS) BUILD RELATIONSHIPS WITH ASSOCIATES (RIM) AND TEACH THEM TO BUILD RELATIONSHIPS WITH CUSTOMERS. ENERGY IS TRANSMITTED TO THE ASSOCIATES AND THE CUSTOMERS THROUGH COMMUNICATION ARCHITECTURE AND GOALS.

The hub of the wheel represents the energy of the company, whether it is top management or the strategy or the cultural ideals. In this case the hub represents the newly created mission, vision, and values. The rim of the wheel represents the people in the organization who meet the public, where the money is generated. The hub can be spinning as fast as lightning, but without a connection to the people who meet the public, nothing happens. The spokes of the wheel transfer the energy from the hub to the rim. They represent the conduits through which communication goes in and out. Dixon pointed out to me that the spokes in a racing wheel are crosshatched to create more speed and efficiency. The spokes represent the managers in the company. When they are crosshatched, they work in tandem rather than in silos. They transfer the energy and momentum to the rim where the "rubber meets the road." Through this graphic I recognized that our pathway to the culture, thus to the profit, lay in the development of the managers and their ability to build relationships.

Caroline had spent the prior six months congealing her ideas for a prosperous furniture company, but she could spin as fast as she wished and would be unable to make the company move without a strong team of connecting spokes.

The communication architecture and our strategic goals enabled managers to transfer the energy of the hub through coaching, education, and empowerment out to the people who touched the customer.

Prepare Your Organization for Change

Within the framework of the architecture, all sorts of changes, big and little can occur because people understand the company, where it is going, why it is changing, and their part to play in executing the changes. ~Caroline

Having witnessed both poorly- and well-executed transitions, we know that changes can be messy and fraught with land mines. Technical and operational transition, even if done well, can be derailed unless a team is prepared for the personal impacts of changes to come. The intangible change of a culture shift may be even more difficult because it necessitates a different mindset for an organization. Preparing to change how people behave is not an easy transition, but critical, because if associates' reactions are unpredictable, results can be unpredictable.

No matter how much we'd like to think otherwise, people don't like change, any change, even an improvement. People may resist the best intentions—the "no good deed goes unpunished" syndrome. We suspect that many at Storehouse were waiting for Caroline to get tired of this culture shift

"First they ignore you, then they fight you and then you win."

Gandhi.

so that they could return to the life they knew, even if they complained about the life they knew. Change can be viewed as far more painful than the pain of the existing conditions, and it doesn't have to be negative to be unsettling to the people who are having their lives altered. Positive change also creates stress for those whose job it is to work with new processes, new people, new goals, and especially new behaviors. People would rather put up with what they have than face the unknown.

A culture change may not appear so difficult—easier than changing business processes, merchandising mix, marketing media, electronic systems. That's a definite maybe. We found it easier to change a sofa design than to change behavior. The management team will be learning a new vocabulary and a new way of managing. Associates may be learning a new relationship with customers and each other, and certainly a new relationship with their managers. This culture shift may change their working lives and have a lasting impact on their personal lives as well.

As with many of our readers, when we launched a major change we could not afford a setback, or even a stall, in our quest for profitability. Based on our experience in leading successful transitions, we present the following systematic plan for strategically directed change management.

Follow the Pathway to Profit in setting the organizational structure.
The first four steps of the pathway build the foundation from which to launch change. Being inclusive in forming the mission, vision, and values, and in the goal setting process, introduces company managers and associates to the new involvement in their own growth. Inclusiveness is an antidote to the painful transition process.

Create a strategy for the changes.
Our new team did not have a skilled merger facilitator, so we hired an expert to organize the transformational architecture. The consultant's job was to make sure we followed our own plan—merge business systems and processes, build our brand through re-merchandised and renamed stores, combine financial reporting, reengineer logistics for greater volume, and train store associates in product knowledge and systems. Combining our knowledge of change management and his facilitation, the transition plan was set in motion. Change opportunities created by the merger allowed us to incorporate the original strategy, a customer-centric company, with the ultimate measure, profit.

> *When you ask people to change you had better have a long-term plan, because if you roll over midway you will have a harder time with your next attempt at change. Avoid the change du jour. It is a credibility and excellence killer. The problem with the idea du jour is that eventually no one believes it will happen and consequently the energy to accomplish new ideas is withheld. The opposite happens when the exercise is a part of a plan, because people become accustomed to achieving goals. Confidence builds. ~Caroline*

Educate managers and associates on the personal effects of change.
Changing a process is easier than changing how people feel about the process. Associates who must implement new ideas will have to do something in a different way, and they will work more successfully if prepared psychologically and technically for the change.

We have seen the big fat books that list every step of the upcoming change, the Gantt charts so carefully prepared, and we are not proposing that they are unnecessary. What we are saying is that the books and charts are not enough. Our new culture was going to change what associates were doing, and our managers needed to understand their reactions to prepare them for the transition looming ahead.

"Prior preparation prevents poor performance" is an old management maxim, and it particularly applies to leading effective change management. Sensitizing or educating your organization to the principles of change, person by person, will eventually develop an organization of individuals who learn not only to react well to change, but will actually drive change proactively. ~Caroline

Build a strong communication architecture.
Communication provides the key to managing change. At Storehouse we started a Transition Newsletter that became an important way to keep associates informed as to our change progress. We established weekly conference calls within departments and a schedule of meetings. Because we communicated so regularly and openly, we alleviated the fear of the unknown. We steeled ourselves to communicate even if the news was not positive. It is tempting to hide bad news hoping that no one notices, or that it can be fixed before it is noticed. At both our companies we were amazed to discover how much people can withstand when they are owners of the process, and equally amazed at how quickly their support can be lost when they perceive that leaders are sandbagging.

Your best arsenal against angst is good facts and figures, combined with your presence, because together they give you the strength to execute the change. Be willing to lose some battles to win the war. ~Caroline

We recognized that building trust was imperative; we had to demonstrate that we would do what we said we would do, and if there was a change we communicated the reason for the change. We believe that adults respond best when they understand why. ~Chris

Prepare for snags by having a strong Plan B.
Despite our best planning process, despite educating our associates, and setting up our communication architecture, everything did not always go according to plan. One example involved technology. We planned a detailed training program to introduce new procedures. We sent the system expert to central locations to train managers, who spent days learning the new system and then taking that knowledge back to their locations to train their associates. On paper it looked like it would work. Once again illustrating that the plan is not as important as the people executing the plan, we found that the system change was succeeding only in frustrating the users. Our reaction was swift and effective. We sent experienced users to every struggling location to work side-by-side with the team. Not only did they learn the system quickly, they learned that we cared enough to give personal attention.

All new processes are messy. ~Caroline

Avoid change piled on change if at all possible.
In an ever-evolving world this may not be possible. When people are off-balance from an ongoing change they are not at their best in embarking on another turn in the road. We found ourselves in that situation at Storehouse and used techniques that actually took advantage of our predicament.

When multiple changes are necessary, group the changes under one umbrella if possible. For example, at Storehouse we were just beginning to shift the culture when we learned that we would be merging two companies. Storehouse was still reeling from changes thrust upon the company by new owners and new leadership. Home Elements was about to lose its identity. The merger became the obvious change, and the culture shift became a part of the merger. We accomplished our vision of building relationships and growing skills as a byproduct of joining the people of two companies.

We took a best-of-the-best approach and did a bottoms-up assessment of the people, the products, the customers, the processes, systems, and the policies. We then worked to create one new, stronger company. From announcement to consummation the exercise took eight months. Overnight the staff began to handle 50% more volume and the engine was revving. A double-digit same-store sales run resulted, and lasted for 30 months. With these sales gains and cost savings due to the merger, our drive to profitability was within our reach.

We had to prioritize and focus on the challenge of the merger although we uncovered other issues that we wanted to fix right away. Heaping change upon change could have derailed our intention.

Keep a "parking lot" of other things you want to work on, and those priorities will bubble up in your strategic and planning process. ~Caroline

Start with a tangible change before venturing into intangible changes.
Starting with a tangible change that responds to a popular request gains support for future intangible culture shifts.

An example of a tangible change at Storehouse that made the intangible easier was our opportunity to update product. New products revitalized everyone—associates and customers. Creating compelling stores produced more customer interest and this was our approach to keeping the workforce excited and engaged while the more difficult areas of changing behavior and attitudes gathered momentum.

Develop the team to seek change proactively.
The factors at play in our quest to seek change proactively:

- ✓ Handling change management from a personal point of view

- ✓ Building on the results we achieved from previous changes

- ✓ Gaining confidence in the strength of our plan

- ✓ Understanding the risk threshold of the team

> *A method of handling change for companies or individuals can be reactive, adaptive, or proactive. My responsibility was to help the organization learn the skills to move from reactive through adaptive to land at the ultimate proactive state. That way we would have a competitive advantage by becoming innovators looking for new ways to embrace, rather than resist change. This process can truly have transformational effects on organizations and people. ~Caroline*

> **The culture also encouraged us to embrace challenge and change, to think of it in a positive way, and I think that has helped me in my life. ~Mary Warner Hart, Storehouse**

During a time of change the old ways don't work any more and the new ways do not feel comfortable. It can be chaotic, but it may become the most creative period in the life of a company.

> *Changing cultural direction can feel like changing the course of a full-steam-ahead ocean liner. It really doesn't want to change course naturally. But that very momentum that resists the initial cultural turn slowly begins to work with you, and before you know it, the culture can be steaming in a new direction. ~Dixon*

Initiate new team members into positive change processes.
I have been asked a question that faces every company. How do you assimilate a new associate to the change process when you have already completed your education on this subject? Being new in a company is being in a change process. The old job has ended, and the associate is not yet comfortable with the new job. That's change. Our process to solve the uncertainty quotient for new people included orientation, development, peer mentoring, coaching, and role modeling. The manager assumed responsibility for including new associates in the team, so we spent our efforts on the manager's skill development. We were also aware that a new associate is likely to emulate someone who appears to know the ropes, so we had to be sure that new associates had good role models.

We needed a systematic plan to affect the behavior of managers that affected the behavior of sales people who affected the customer, and the patience to do it in an orderly fashion, continuing existing processes so that our profits didn't suffer as we changed. It was much like hopping on a rolling train, or trying to change the propeller on a plane in midair during a rainstorm. ~Caroline

Shape Your Infrastructure

Unmanaged energy in a company is anarchy, having the capability of pulling the organization apart. The leader is responsible for focusing the energy flow in a positive direction. Leaders identify boundaries within which people can operate. The visionary keeps moving the borders as the company and the associates grow. The talent is to know how quickly to move those borders. ~Caroline

For real change to take place constructively, a good foundation had to be in place. As we worked on sensitizing the individual we worked on corporate structure. Coaching, empowerment, and education—representing the means by which the essence of the mission, vision, and values permeates the organization—surround the hub of our wheel. If managers were to become the connection to the associates we needed to construct an effective communications and development architecture through which the coaching, empowerment, and education could be executed. Our communication architecture was designed to align three elements of our message:

1.   The way we stayed in touch

2.   The way we built skills

3.   The way we recognized achievement

1. The way we stayed in touch

We see two-way communication as a key to the inclusiveness that creates loyalty, collaboration, and ownership. Our geographically challenged companies taught us to set the expectation and means to communicate, otherwise some managers would revert to silo management and associates would revert to isolated individuals who didn't identify with the company.

Good communicators realize there are three parts of effective communication: speaking, listening, and hearing. ~Chris

I have found in my career that a company that nurtures its talent and shares information not only from the top down, but from the bottom up, is a company more likely to have actively engaged staff and customers. ~Jennifer Spencer, This End Up

Examples of communication opportunities:

✓ Coordinated meetings. These were both departmental and cross departmental meetings to solve problems, plan future activities, provide information, educate, and celebrate achievements. In addition to the topics on the agenda, coordinated meetings also solidified relationships within and between departments. The ownership that comes through involvement is priceless.

✓ Conference calls, video conferences, Skype, etc. Since we were a geographically challenged company, technology provided another way to communicate. For example, our weekly district conference calls allowed managers to take an hour and connect with their peers. At the end of the conference call Chris set up individual phone times with each member of the team to provide opportunities for them to voice their needs. A listening schedule ensured that the communication habit was formed.

✓ Newsletters. At Storehouse our newsletter began as a means to keep people informed about the merger we were undertaking, and continued because it reminded everyone that we were a team. It featured information, motivation, and recognition. Having one's name in print increases ownership equity.

✓ Email. We used email as a quick and easy way to get critical information to everyone at the same time. Operational or merchandising changes that needed immediate attention could be done within the day.

✓ Social media. Companies use social media to connect people to the brand and it has become a primary avenue for networking, marketing, and recruiting.

✓ Snail mail. We still see a place for snail mail in our corporate communication structure. I once used our mail to send notes of congratulations to managers who made their goals each month. These were just scribbled on small slips of paper, so imagine my surprise when one manager told me that she had all of them posted and they inspired her to do her best every day. It became her goal to get one of my scribbled notes each month. In this culture recognition does not hinge on the amount of money spent, but the personal action taken when there is an opportunity for praise.

Snail mail has become a more impressive way to communicate because it has become so rare. The recipient sees evidence of effort in the selection of paper, locating a pen, composing the note, looking up the address and finding a stamp, not to mention getting the note to the post office. ~Dixon

Information is a key component in empowerment. The formal communication architecture ensures that the teams and the individuals stay aligned with organizational goals. ~Caroline

2. The way we built skills

With the framework and opportunity for communication established, we began to strengthen our culture through the development of our team. Few of the managers or associates had been a part of a company that emphasized individual development leading to corporate success. Although they appreciated the concept, they had no prior experience in building such an environment. We invested in training and development and they learned to achieve their goals through individual growth.

In working with managers and associates we realized that although they were familiar with training, they were not familiar with development. We view training as an event project with a beginning, middle, and end. A company might train someone to enter an order in a computer system or change a tire. We view development as a process that never ends. It includes training, but is steeped in manager-associate interaction. It is usually participative and results in change, often in both manager and associate. It could be a change in thinking, in attitude, in behavior, in outlook, in perspective, any of those life-altering transitions. Development does not typically occur without the associate's acceptance. In the Culture of Caring the development never ends, even for the leader.

A training workshop may energize and motivate, but the true measure of successful development is observing a behavior change. ~Chris

We found that by coordinating these methods our training sessions evolved into development:

- ✓ Workshops. We began a series of coordinated workshops to teach communication, leadership, customer relations, and other topics that supported the company mission. A list of workshops is included in the Addendum.

- ✓ Coaching. We introduced a positive coaching style that focused on self-reflection. Willingness to coach directly correlated with successful execution. We started with the managers because they drove the cultural changes.

- ✓ Common language. As we taught workshops and coached we developed words and phrases that became a communication shortcut to ideas and principles.

- ✓ Counseling. We learned to give honest communication in a positive way and to address problems through a root-cause analysis method.

- ✓ Performance reviews. We encouraged individuals to evaluate their own performance by having them come to review meetings prepared to discuss their own achievements and opportunities for improvement.

- ✓ Action planning. Individuals and departments determined the tactics employed for success. Helping them align individual actions with company goals was more effective than dictating assignments.

- ✓ Participation. Encouraging managers and associates to take part in workshops, lead sessions, and teach new associates became a source of growth and energy. Participation creates ownership. Ownership produces profit.

Many organizations consider some of these skills to be "soft stuff," but the truth is that the skills needed to master the soft stuff are the hardest to learn. Addressing the soft stuff can be a competitive advantage because most companies don't even try to understand it.

> *"Anticipation creates participation."*
>
> *Karen McNeill, owner, McNeill Communications Group Inc.*

3. The way we recognized achievement

In addition to our communication structure and development program, we aligned our recognition and compensation programs to reward the desired results.

One of our challenges at Storehouse was how to compensate and motivate a sales force, combining individual performance with team performance. Our sales associates were accustomed to a commission structure. In their "I" centered selling environment, individual commissions were quite motivating. As we moved to a "we" selling environment centered on the customer, we worked with finance and human resources to set up a compensation program to link group achievement and individual initiative.

Another example: This End Up devised a program for delivery drivers to earn bonus dollars based on excellence in service.

Other ways we recognized excellent performance:

✓ Acknowledgement of accomplishment—an order saved, a cost avoided, a new manager developed, a happy customer

✓ Recognition at the annual business meeting

✓ Reward trip for top performers

✓ Name in print in the bi-weekly newsletter

✓ Gift for breaking sales records

✓ Dinner with the president for the store setting a company sales record

✓ Behind the scenes award

✓ Handwritten thank you notes

✓ Semi-annual contest to reward creativity in merchandising

I don't think our visual managers fully understood their responsibility until we initiated a semi-annual contest/review of their work, judged by their peers, and rewarded for achievement. ~Dixon

The most amazing example of pride in receiving recognition is the image I remember of This End Up's strong, burly delivery drivers whose hats were weighed down with "golden arrow" pins received because they had been complimented in a customer letter.

. . . To have a company where the VP will actually personally recognize individual performers has never left me. I [now] manage almost 100 people at any one time and I learned . . . the importance of saying thank you, and great job. I still will write thank you notes to members of the team. ~Jennifer Spencer, This End Up

Manage by Values and Success Principles

What does this culture look like in action? When it is working you will see this: core leaders creating the cultural environment consciously rather than by accident. There is a cause and effect of everything they do, in their humor, recognition, and counseling. Through awareness that they are creating something, they ensure it is what they want. ~Caroline

We see the culture as a part of the strategy to achieve profits. Most business consultants would say that strategy is key to business success. In addition to strategy, we had measurable goals. Strategy and goals are important, but we knew that we would not succeed based on strategy and goals alone.

FIGURE# 5 COMPANY GOALS AND CULTURAL GOALS SUPPORT FINANCIAL GOALS.

When you knit together a group of people with common ideals and goals and they apply common values, it unleashes the cultural energy that manages for you when no one is looking. Your company's values are the foot soldiers that work for you when you are not there. ~Caroline

Caroline tells a story of being a sales associate earning a whopping $3.15/ hour. She remembers standing in her kitchen late one night on the phone with a dissatisfied customer. Pay had nothing to do with her willingness to work through the issue. She did it because she felt that she counted. The president knew her name. People were depending on her—the culture at work when no one is looking.

> *"The fact is, culture eats strategy for lunch."*
>
> *Merck CEO, Dick Clark*

We found that by working according to our values we attracted people for whom these values created success, and others either didn't care to join us or left because the expectation was so uncomfortable. It helped us to keep the quality of excellence in our membership. Excellent people want to work with excellent people.

Living the values

> *Be intentional. Imagine the environment you want. Write about it, speak about it, and put your words into action. Then measure your results and course correct until you achieve your goals. People are always watching their managers to gain clues as to how they should behave. We are never perfect at living the values; we just aspire to them.* ~Caroline

In collaboratively creating Storehouse's value statements, we had taken the first step toward making them practical tools. When faced with critical decisions, the managers and associates weighed values to help shape solutions. The values became tools to guide decision-making and how to treat people.

To be certain that our managers knew how to handle each situation, we introduced them to the reality of working in a company environment managed by the values we had agreed would guide us. The managers may have worked under rules in other companies and they may have worked with little attention or support, but few had ever worked in an environment that must mirror the values our company professed. Even though they had authored the words, words alone will not make a company culture. We had to live the culture we wanted. From our experience we knew that the managers create the environment. It may sound trite, but the only way I knew to build the culture we wanted was to "walk the talk." What does the walk look like?

> *One of my favorite sayings is "Leaders do not get the luxury of having a bad day in public."* ~Chris

To help managers see the importance of their role in perpetuating the values, we developed a workshop to demonstrate what actions followed the culture through all the phases of an associate's career.

We divided our workshop into the life cycle of employment—selection/hiring, new employee training, good performance, times when performance is not good, and the separation process. We were pleased to note that the managers were aware of the steps they must take to live the values in each situation and I needed to do very little other than gather the ideas. Maybe this was not always their practice, but they knew what actions reflected the culture. Using their ideals I was able to develop workshops to teach the skills needed to manage to the cultural expectations.

Could we have saved the expense and time by developing the guidelines ourselves? Of course. Yet, this is another example where inclusiveness and participation increases the probability of ownership of results.

People want to grow, feel like they matter and are recognized; they want good relationships with their manager and peers. If you can harness this thought you can tap into the invisible currency of an organization. ~Caroline

Making emotional deposits

Our workshop also introduced the concept of the "emotional deposit" compared by author Stephen Covey to deposits in a bank account. At This End Up we had discovered the magic of emotional deposits because there were times when we had to ask for extra effort, a sacrifice of time, a difficult situation to handle, or some other request that could be viewed as "not my job." In other words, we needed to make a withdrawal. We were able to withdraw from that emotional bank account because we had made so many deposits there.

Like any good bank account, you have to put in before you withdraw. ~Dixon

Our managers volunteered ideas of what they could do to contribute to the development of their associates. Many managers expect associates to work to win their favor. However, it has been our observation that the most successful managers create a positive emotional bond with their associates by helping the associates to achieve their goals and the company goals. And, by most successful, I am not speaking of just the most popular managers, but the most profitable.

These emotional deposits can be different for different people. For some people it is recognition, for others an unexpected gift, some react to additional responsibility, and others want to be included in what is considered important. Most just want attention. In our workshop the ideas flowed so quickly that it was difficult to capture them all. We identified over 80 actions that could be emotional deposits.

Emotional deposits and attention create mind pictures, but a story sent in by this former associate adds a delicious aroma and mouthwatering anticipation to the picture.

"Attention is to people as fertilizer is to flowers."

~Dixon's Granny Kemp

As a grammar school child my family and I lived close to the school. . . . A bakery was located across from the schoolyard. I vividly remember my mom slipping me a

warm cookie through the fence at recess one day. This was the essence of my [Culture of Caring] experience, 'the warm cookie' factor . . . I own a small hobby show business selling jewelry and bags. I strive to offer good service and good product at fair prices and have fun with what I do. I always have plenty of warm cookies and use them wisely. ~Sandy Kohut MacDonald, This End Up

Emotional deposit can come from the entire company.

On August 27 of last year (2005) I packed a backpack with three days worth of clothes to leave New Orleans to go to my parents' house for what I thought would be a weekend evacuation while yet another hurricane blew through New Orleans. It wasn't going to be a big deal, just like the others that had come close in the past four years. I wasn't worried. Maybe I was a little irritated, but that was about it. As you all know, Katrina proceeded to destroy the city I lived in, flooding both my home and the store in Metairie. For a month I wasn't even allowed back into my neighborhood. And when I met the insurance adjuster at the . . . store, the roof had been ripped off and there was at least a half a foot of flooding. Needless to say, I wasn't sure what I was going to do. My entire life had been washed away. But Storehouse did not turn its back on me. So many of my friends from New Orleans lost their jobs and had no options other than to relocate to find work, or to stay in the city trying to find something to help them by. Storehouse and our employees did so much more.

People from all over the company donated money and vacation time so that my co-workers and I (all eight of us) were able to continue to be paid and to maintain our health care benefits for several months. We were all offered the opportunity to relocate temporarily, which some of us did, and we were all assured that we would have our jobs back when the store reopened. And we all did. I was the only one who chose to make my relocation permanent. Not only did Storehouse do more than I could have ever expected, Storehouse did more than any other company I have heard about. ~Michael Norris, Storehouse

What benefit did the company derive from the emotional deposit we made with these eight people in New Orleans? When the store reopened, we had a fully trained and empathetic staff ready to assist customers who had suffered the same losses of home and furnishings that plagued the whole city.

Understanding your employee's personal goals, missions, and moti-vations helps you to find the right emotional deposit for that indi-vidual. ~Caroline

Managing across boundaries

In the Culture of Caring company ownership requires everyone to work for solutions. It is not enough to report a problem up-line, file a complaint. When the culture is working, people solve issues together. We learned how to approach each other—someone from another department, a peer, maybe even our managers. Handling the issue on the spot can prevent escalation and it can be a developmental opportunity—for both parties.

> **I spent 5 years facilitating home office orientation. . . . I once had someone approach me, saying, 'You know how you talk about honest communication, and to just do it? Well, I need to talk to you about X' and it was something I genuinely appreciated them discussing with me, because I think it helped BOTH of us grow, and I got to see the shared values—the ones I had shared with them—put into action in a very positive way. The issue itself was minor—it was the seeing of the values being lived that was so powerful. ~Barbara Ross, This End Up**

The managers' actions set the stage for the environment. No statement expounding the value of people in an organization would ring true unless every manager demonstrated the culture with every contact. For the culture to be strong, both managers and associates had to be able to picture the values in practical application.

Understand Yourself and Others

Our company will become an incubator for leaders. Our environment will attract and retain the best and the brightest in our field. ~Caroline

When Caroline spoke these words, she was sharing a vision, certainly not a reality at the time.

A critical part of the Pathway to Profit includes the creation of a management program to develop the skills and talents of leaders. We could not bestow a title and expect the results to follow. Authority is easy to delegate, while the ability to influence takes skill.

When people feel cared about, they demonstrate more caring for those around them, and for their customers. When customers feel this kind of ownership they respond, and a positive cycle of relationships is unleashed. Caring requires the commitment to build a trusting and open environment that promotes diversity in all forms, including thought. Caring also requires honest performance management and holding teammates accountable for results.

"The key to successful leadership today is influence, not authority."

Author, Ken Blanchard

Caring leadership helps create an environment where people want to work on their weaknesses. Honest constructive criticism, given in the spirit of helping one improve, builds confidence and self-esteem and produces very different results than operating from blame. Caring leaders try to understand their associates' viewpoints. We all know at some level what each other is thinking; by communicating openly and honestly we build trust. ~Caroline

The passion that the leaders at Storehouse had for coaching, giving feedback, and understanding communication styles is evident in every aspect of my career. Where I use it often is in my one-on-ones with my leadership team. . . . If I do not seek to understand them, they will never care to understand me. ~Christy Carpenter, Storehouse

We knew that by practicing the Culture of Caring we would enable our managers to manage by influence rather than by authority alone. While we recognized their talent and experience, we also had the difficult task of holding up the mirror so that they could see themselves as their teams saw them. Our Culture of Caring depended upon our managers being able to self-reflect and self-correct because their behavior was the model for their associates. Many of our managers had no exposure to a management philosophy other than establishing authority.

Our belief is that it is the actual positive, caring, constructive relationship between the manager and associate that gets the cycle moving and the flywheel spinning. So, for our company to reach its customers through the associates, we set up a process for continually improving the relationship between associates and managers.

Habit #5 "Seek first to understand, then to be understood."

Stephen Covey, The 7 Habits of Highly Effective People

To have the leaders we needed, we would have to develop them in what Caroline calls our "leadership incubator."

We selected four key components for our launch:

1. Change management practices

2. Communication style

3. Conflict management style

4. Leadership style

> "We know that the foundation of every great workplace is trust between employees and management."
>
> Great Place to Work® Institute

With the understanding of these four components our managers would be able to build the Culture of Caring environment for the people on their teams.

Specific characteristics create a trusting environment: consistency, accountability, follow through, clear goals, inclusiveness, and an understanding of each person's part to play. Leaders must be confidential and discreet. When our managers first realized that our environment was changing they thought we would back off; only when we kept going did they understand the value of the changes. It takes years. You think it has taken hold, but if you relax your focus, you may return to find it is not still there. ~Caroline

1. Change management practices

Change is always viewed by the individual with this question, "How does it affect me?" ~Dixon

The merger of two companies so early in our culture shift required that we begin our leadership development program with a change workshop, so managers could understand the transition process experienced by individuals who faced change. A book by William Bridges, *Managing Transition, Making the Most of Change*, became a valuable tool and we gave each manager a copy.

People need to see the benefit to them for making the changes they are asked to make—enlightened self-interest. ~Chris

A systematic plan to affect the behavior of managers affects the behavior of associates. And, whatever affects associates, eventually affects customers. A vital and healthy company is making changes; however, what appears trivial to executives may seem monumental to associates who have to alter what they do every day. I remember when our drivers switched from wearing their own clothes to uniforms. We initiated the new look at one warehouse by discussing the benefit to the driver. With their strong approval, the change was a positive move. A problem occurred when the drivers at other centers were disgruntled with the change because they weren't included in the transition process. The contrast in response illustrates the importance of considering how a change will affect associates.

When managers learned about the transition that accompanies change they were able to guide their teams through a change process. The language we used in the workshop became a part of our corporate lingo, so that over the years we were able to recall change principles with a few short phrases. One colleague wrote that she remembered an exercise we did at our workshop.

> **I have used that 'Change Exercise' you did with us years ago with the picture selection, and the emotion that resonated. ~Cathy Caples, Storehouse**

> *The work happened over months and years, and layer upon layers of development helped to deepen the understanding. Our teammates developed a vocabulary around change and the process. And finally the culture took shape. It took skill, wisdom, determination, and perseverance, and it wasn't pretty at first, I can assure you. ~Caroline*

A personal sidebar: I experienced significant changes as both our companies were navigating against outside pressures. Because I understood and had taught the dynamics of change, I thought that I had it all under control. Surely I would not experience the emotional upheavals that people tend to go through when they are in the throes of transition. Not so. Knowing where I was in the process of adjusting to change did not mean that I didn't experience the emotion; it just meant I knew where I was and why. And somehow that helped me.

> *Our change management education gave me the tools to understand the process of what was happening to me, so I was more emotionally prepared to lead through the tough changes. ~Caroline*

2. Communication style

Creating a communication structure is essential, but structure alone will not ensure effective communication. We taught a course to identify individual communication styles and learn how to relate to other styles, enabling the manager to connect, solve problems, and get stronger results. Understanding provided the foundation of strong relationships. Strong relationships provided the foundation for an empowered culture. The empowered culture drove profit.

While there are many respected and validated tools and experts in the field of communication, we choose the Myers-Briggs Type Indicator® program to develop those skills in managers. It is well documented and validated; there is no right or wrong, good or bad; and it teaches how to communicate in other people's styles.

We worked with our managers to identify their own preferences and appreciate the different preferences of others; then we began to work on how their own communication style affected others.

Communication was our first venture into the practice of self-discovery at Storehouse and we had several managers tell us after the workshop that they had answered the questions on the instrument to appear as they thought people in their jobs should be. During the workshop they discovered their true communication styles. We were not surprised because we knew we had not yet earned their trust that the culture was nonjudgmental. This realization brought growth in terms of self-reflection. Under stress we communicate in our natural preference, so taking that first step in accepting themselves as they were allowed them to build the skills to vary the style for the appropriate situation.

I like to begin management introspection with this communication workshop because it sets the stage for easy interaction. I have never held a communication workshop that was not punctuated with fun and laughter. Since there is no right or wrong, we can all end the class feeling good about ourselves. We took what we had learned about our own communication styles and the styles of the people we managed and learned how to use this information in effective communication for our associates' development. It is a powerful tool.

Effective communication requires acceptance of the other person's preference—respect for diversity.

> I have had two jobs since leaving . . . and knowing my [communication] type has been invaluable. Because of it, I definitely have more patience when dealing with others, especially those who are totally opposite. ~Debbie Robbins, Storehouse

In more hierarchical management environments the manager's preference becomes the rule of the day. Associates show deference by adapting to the manager's style. The most enlightened managers are those who communicate in the style of those they manage, rather than demanding adherence to their own preference. We call it "getting to where the other person is," a key ingredient in gaining the willing cooperation of others to achieve results.

Practice sessions are valuable in learning to use the communication tool. When we coached the managers in real-life management issues, we talked about communication preferences and integrated this process into an effective problem-solving approach.

It was like turning on a light. Suddenly our communication strengths and growth areas were illuminated. This knowledge helped us tap into our strengths and develop strategies for minimizing our potential pitfalls. For example, my team realized we had the tendency to make decisions too quickly. Knowing this, we invested more time in gathering facts and analyzing data before we came to a decision. ~Chris

> **The Myers-Briggs training . . . was, and continues to be, such a valuable tool to me. . . . Communication with people is so key and so valuable in building strong relationships.**
> **~Kathy Tierney, This End Up and Storehouse**

3. Conflict management style

In any culture, management is about solving problems and initiating strategic changes through people. Dissonance is a sidekick of change. In the Culture of Caring, the ability to manage and grow through addressing dissonant situations is critical to the empowered culture. Learning positive conflict management techniques enabled managers to use difficult situations to develop associates in a positive environment. And it gave us an organization that harnessed problem solving as a pathway to profit.

Success comes from rooting out problems and solving them, and managers rarely do that without some conflict.

Our mentor, Stewart Brown, knew that deep lessons are learned through surface disagreements and that new ideas emerged which wouldn't have been discovered without the motivation of dissonance. He always looked for an alternative path and we called this process "discovering the third right way."

We learned the strength of the debate. Stewart taught us to disagree and still maintain respect for each other. Because our debates had positive results we became confident to wade in quickly, before anger was an issue. This ability and knowledge to address conflict early allowed us to face our brutal realities without fear. The result of healthy debate evolved into active engagement and a sense of ownership. Our ideas were important, even if they differed.

Knowing that under stress we automatically revert to our innate conflict management style, we needed an instrument for managers to discover how they actually reacted in conflict. For our workshop we chose the Thomas-Kilmann conflict management principles, using their terminology for five different ways of handling conflict with the appropriate style for a given situation—"avoiding, accommodating, competing, compromising, and collaborating"—and discussed how to apply them in difficult interactions. We're not talking about war; we were examining how we handled differences of opinion, or a heated discussion.

We observe that people often don't address conflicts because a lack of skill can produce a negative response, which starts a vicious cycle. However, a success with a conflict situation builds the confidence to break the cycle. Teaching skills was our key to ensuring that success.

The biggest surprise to our group was the fallibility of compromise, which we had all assumed to be the ultimate goal of conflict resolution. Not necessarily so. While each of the five styles has the optimum application, the most powerful style turned out to be collaboration, the style we had called "the third right way." Collaboration may be the most difficult to employ, but results in a win for both factions. We learned to look past the opposing sides and find the third option that would meet the needs of both parties. We used collaboration in goal setting, performance enhancement, individual growth, and conflict resolution.

> *The concept of finding the third option caught on and we got to a point where conflicting individuals began their discussion with the search for the third idea. ~Chris*

While our managers learned the importance of addressing conflict, we also shared another of Stewart's wise instincts—there are times that even avoidance is a good conflict management technique. Some problems solve themselves if monitored, but left alone.

4. Leadership style
Our goal to be a leadership incubator required us to educate our managers about the different roles of leaders, giving them the understanding and tools to be effective.

My favorite book on leadership is Daniel Goleman's *Primal Leadership, Realizing the Power of Emotional Intelligence*. Goleman describes six styles of leadership—"visionary, coaching, affiliative, democratic, pacesetting, and commanding."

> *Learning leadership styles gives you the tools to be effective in different situations. Knowing your "shoes off" style and being aware of other styles, you understand the situation, then you can choose the most effective leadership. ~Caroline*

In order to study leadership in a self-reflective manner, I created an instrument to help managers identify their personal leadership style. The instrument had not been officially tested, nor did I have statistics to prove its reliability, but it was a tool to help our managers see how their associates perceived their leadership style. Once they understood the attributes of each style, they were able to identify their preferences. We looked at this openness as a good indication of how astute they had become about holding up the mirror for themselves.

In addition to the skills we learned, we discovered the value of working in small groups, joining people who trusted one another and were not shy about helping their teammates to see themselves as others saw them. Mutual respect among their peer group caused them to be more comfortable with different styles and created a willingness to work together to determine the most appropriate leadership style for the situation.

All of the time invested in our leadership culture really paid off. ~Kim Britt, Storehouse

As we taught managers to recognize their own natural leadership style they learned which style would emerge unbidden in times of stress. We also gained a terminology to be used company-wide in talking about how leaders handle problems. At this point we could speak in a new vocabulary for change, communication, conflict, and leadership styles.

Our development programs on communication, change, conflict management, and leadership gave us structure and a shared vocabulary so we could focus on solving the problem or situation rather than focusing on the personalities involved. We were able to cut through a lot of rhetoric and get to the root cause of a problem more quickly. ~Chris

Teach conflict, communications, and management skills when times are good and you don't have to use them, so that you have a common method and vocabulary to address issues when needed. ~Caroline

Connect the Culture to the Customer

Our value model illustrates that our key competitive difference would be to create exceptional shopping experiences for our customers. Superior service would set us apart in our style, price, and design category. ~Caroline

While we were busy developing management skills to create the working environment for our associates, we were ever mindful of the need to enhance the shopping experience for our customers. Every business has a customer, an end user for product or service. The point of the Culture of Caring is delivering a better experience for customers, increasing business and resulting in profits.

We evaluated avenues to business success—product, price, and service. Although we were committed to good design in product and offering value at a mid-price point, we knew that our competitive advantage must be in our service. Our connection to the customer needed to surpass all competition. Excellent service depended on a strong foundation:

- ✓ Our associates needed to know their product and service offerings.

- ✓ Our operations needed to be streamlined.

- ✓ We needed a customer-centric selling program.

- ✓ We needed to provide product or service that our competition did not offer.

- ✓ We needed to create successful outcomes for customer issues.

Create Your Selling Environment

Our challenge was to balance the refined, sophisticated styling of our store appearance with the warmth of our sales team. The store itself made the style statement. We needed to develop the friendly neighborhood store environment, engaging all customers in the design process of creating beautiful rooms. We wanted every sale, so we needed to dispel any hint of aloofness as soon as the customer entered the store.

We identified four major shifts to enrich the customer experience:

1. Switch the focus from product to customer.

2. Mirror the buying process with the selling process.

3. Develop selling skills to make good design accessible and increase revenue.

4. Educate associates in design principles to offer consulting service to customers.

1. Switch the focus from product to customer.
At This End Up we realized that the product is not as important as the people who use it. That philosophy changed the way we related to customers and we knew that Storehouse would benefit if we shifted from product focus to customer focus. Our working hypothesis of customer-centricity was derived from the selling skills of This End Up, developed all those years ago by Libby, Caroline, Dixon, and the other innovative managers. Chris, having been the company champion of selling skills, had those skills firmly engrained in her mind. But, as we recommend in our Pathway, we took our working hypothesis and called together a taskforce of sales practitioners from each Storehouse district. Our question to them was: "What is your vision of the ideal customer experience?"

We knew where we wanted to be, but we needed the group to participate in getting there. ~Chris

Customer-centricity was as clear as fog when Chris and I worked with this committee of managers, and as foreign to them as a new language, but they did understand that increasing our sales would offer up opportunities for revenue. We charted their ideas of the optimum customer experience from the time the customer entered the store until the sale was completed. As we had previously experienced with gathering ideas for our mission, vision, and values, the group identified with the experiences they wanted as customers and we were right on target with our hypothesis. We were confident that we could shape the outcome if necessary, but again it wasn't necessary. They knew the ingredients of a good customer experience; they just didn't know how to make it happen consistently in their stores.

For example, we knew that the customers we attracted to our stores did not always experience a welcoming environment, that we were not yet the friendly neighborhood store. We also knew that if we confronted the managers with that observation we would jeopardize our opportunity to gain buy-in. Imagine our amazement when the managers at the taskforce initiated a poll, asking themselves how many customers in their stores were not greeted. They estimated that over half of the people walking into our stores were never even acknowledged. Stifling our groans and without our having to lecture, it became obvious to all that we could increase our sales if we changed our selling environment.

From that self-initiated breakthrough we were able to garner their buy-in to try something new.

Including key opinion leaders in the development of new programs is valuable for several reasons. Not only do they offer insight and perspective, they become partners in promoting the benefits of change to the larger group. ~Chris

How hard could it be to greet every customer? To our everlasting surprise, it was one of the hardest mountains we had to climb. We were able to achieve a "Hello," or "What are you looking for today?" But customer-centric selling, to greet customers as people we were glad to see, rather than potential orders, that was more difficult than we anticipated. We learned that we needed to teach the art of conversation because some associates were not accustomed to starting a conversation with a customer. Our sales leaders learned that the art of conversation could be profitable.

A former This End Up store manager has built a successful real estate career in the years since the close of her store. She told me that she still keeps in contact with her former store customers, and when their paths cross, her customers remember her. Ten years after buying furniture, who remembers the person who sold it? There is no doubt in my mind as to why she has been successful in real estate.

We were creating the environment for the exceptional customer experience by teaching our sales associates to build a bond with the customer through the art of conversation. The skills needed to build relationships within the company are the same skills needed to build relationships with customers.

2. Mirror the buying process with the selling process.

Our selling program was built from the customer's point of view because our question to the taskforce was "What is your vision of the ideal customer experience?" and their comments were from the customer's perspective. Our working session produced a graphic depicting the customer experience and the associate's role in that experience, giving us a comprehensive outline of the behavioral skills it would take to create our ideal store environment. We were then able to take their ideas, meld them with selling principles, and come up with a fresh approach, unique to Storehouse. No other training program duplicated our style of working with customers.

From this basic graphic design we developed the entire sales training program. We coordinated the skills to recognize where customers were in the buying process with the skills to maximize the selling opportunities in each transaction. Although the managers had shaped the selling program, I have to say that our experience in changing behavior resembled changing that propeller in mid-flight.

3. Develop selling skills for making good design accessible and increased revenue.

I laugh when I think back to my first years managing a team. I did think my team would just naturally do what they saw me doing. It was quite an "aha" moment when I realized this was not the case and I had better get about the work of training and coaching. ~Chris

Our managers became coaches because we believe that the manager in any business focused on the development of associates creates a stronger, more productive team, positioned for profit. Associates bond with the person who helps them grow and gain the recognition that comes with increased productivity.

Other companies may arm their managers with rules and checklists, expecting consistent results to come from consistent corrective application. Although we didn't try to eliminate all rules and checklists, we did prioritize education and development as a critical role of a manager. Several advantages came from broadening their role:

✓ The manager-coaches had a vested interest in the success of the associates.

✓ The manager's skills improved through teaching their associates.

✓ The manager/associate relationship strengthened.

✓ The manager was more involved with customer interaction.

> *Coaching results rather than using checklist management requires time, patience, and skill. Managers coming from an operational culture were challenged to develop this skill and to trust that they would get to a better result. ~Chris*

The concept of coaching everyone in the store on a daily basis increased selling skills, but our managers needed help in coaching. We found that managers didn't coach because they viewed coaching as a conflict situation and they lacked the skill to coach in a positive manner. Or, they thought that they had hired professionals who didn't need to be taught anything.

We believe that the secret to building an effective coaching session is for the coach to "ask, don't tell." That sounds easy enough, but in application telling is a tough habit to break. Because coaching was focused on self-discovery, the associates could even coach each other. As they learned that there was no critical judgment, associates became more comfortable using coaching as a developmental process.

> *One of the challenges we faced was getting buy-in that coaching was an asking, not telling, process. It seemed easier to tell people what they needed to improve, and how to do it. It took many hours of "coaching the coach" on the sales floor before we saw this change. When we observed behavior changes on the sales floor, we knew the associate had bought in to the customer-centric approach. ~Chris*

> **Hi Anita, When I first met you I wasn't quite sure. Who is this and what is she talking about?? By golly, you know your business!! I loved every [sales training class], I loved every time we got together. . . . The strength and the ability you gave me to coach in a way I have never done before was amazing. I look forward to using these principles in my next endeavors. ~Sharon Schmitz, Storehouse**

Were we successful in establishing our customer-relations philosophy? This is a letter we received from a store manager:

> **What made Storehouse different from the rest of the retail furniture world was its approach to the business environment. We as a company did not chase credit cards or cash. . . . We established relationships. The**

relationships were between clients and design consultants and relationships between all employees, whether they be logistics, corporate, management, or design consultants. . . . In a happy work environment the customers are always taken care of in the best possible way. The key word in [our] philosophy was RELATIONSHIPS. ~Elizabeth McKernan, Storehouse

We were using these selling and leadership programs to move the goal a little further each time, building confidence and self esteem that in the beginning seemed a little out of reach. ~Caroline

4. Educate associates in design principles to offer consulting service to customers.

In our quest to increase our competitive advantage we offered complimentary design service for our customers. Buying furniture is a scary process for many customers considering the challenge of coordinating fabrics, styles, and colors, so they appreciate the expert's assurance that they have selected wisely. Very few furniture retail stores offered this service on a complimentary basis. Initially we had a number of store associates who were educated in design and we began considering that skill in our hiring process. For the others we offered design certification through the Interior Design Society. When we learned that our associates and managers were finding it difficult to complete the course without a class structure, we developed design classes to be included in our workshops. These classes became so popular that we developed half-hour design courses that could be taught by any store manager or associate in a store meeting Combined with our customer-focused selling, our design service was creating the friendly neighborhood store that made good design readily accessible.

We found more success when education programs were accomplished in a team setting. ~Caroline

Create Successful Outcomes for Customer Issues

When responding to a customer who is angry with your company's product or service, be aware of the thoughts that you are harboring in your own mind, because you can be sure that your response will reflect your thoughts, either in words or intonation. ~Caroline

This End Up did not have a customer service department because Stewart Brown believed that we all should be ambassadors and support the customer, himself included. And he did take customer calls. In fact, he was an expert and we all learned from him. Didn't he have other things to do? Of course, but Stewart realized that he had no company without customers. He saw his role as support for those who supported the customer. Living this philosophy brought him a very profitable business.

I was head of human resources and if the receptionist couldn't find the appropriate person for the call, I took it. The customer only had to tell the story once, making the problem easier to solve, a solution that is always a balance between the customer's interests and the company's interests. Done well it is a win for the customer and a win for the company.

In our Pathway to Profit, learning to create successful outcomes for customer issues would ideally come after we had established our selling environment, but necessity dictated that we learn to solve problems at the same time we were learning to build our customer base.

> *At This End Up we all bought into the notion that the customer was critically important to our business. To emphasize this idea we capitalized the word "Customer" in all our written communication and we taught associates to ask, "Are you with a customer?" anytime they called a store during business hours. These might sound like insignificant actions but they underscored the value we placed on service. ~Chris*

We took our customer service style with us to Storehouse, but found that things were done very differently there. District sales managers were responsible for resolving all customer issues. That had worked well for them as long as volumes were small and issues were limited. As we proceeded with the merger at Storehouse, that same distribution center problem we described earlier began to impact our sales team. Volume at the center increased drastically as they absorbed deliveries for the former Home Elements stores in addition to a larger number of Storehouse stores. Plus, with new product choices, our sales had increased. Good news all around, except that the center was not organized to handle the volume. While Christina, our CFO, worked with distribution and technology to organize the center for twice their usual volume, we needed to address the unhappy customers who were not experiencing our usual competent service. They were all directed to call our district managers. We had to unchain those six managers from their cell phones if we were ever going to get them on the sales floor developing our selling strength.

Understanding that the Pathway to Profit is an iterative process, we immediately began to teach associates how to handle customer issues.

Our vision portrayed our customers as being so impressed with their experience at Storehouse that they told their friends and family what a great company we were. Clearly we had not achieved that vision if we had not handled their orders to their satisfaction. Our challenge was to teach every store manager and associate the skill of handling issues before they escalated. We recommended that whoever answered the phone or greeted the customer handle the problem, unless the customer's primary contact was readily available. This practice ensured that the customer only had to tell the story once. Anyone who has ever had to make multiple calls to resolve a problem will probably remember that the frustration level accelerated with each repeat of the problem. As a business we were more likely to be able to resolve the issue without excessive expense if our customer was not frustrated. Our seasoned managers looked at me as though I spoke a foreign language when I taught them how to handle angry people.

It may seem a stretch to presume that people are empowered by teaching them to handle customer situations, but having lived the concept of universal responsibility for the customer, we are convinced that handling issues for customers builds a feeling of ownership. We used the example of Caroline's story as a sales associate standing in her kitchen at night dealing with a customer issue. She wasn't a manager at the time, but we know that owning this customer problem was a step toward her management career.

The Culture of Caring instilled three basic tenets that would change the mindset of associates who handled customer situations.

1. Imagine yourself in the customer's place.
One of our managers later admitted that she thought I was operating in la-la land, but she went back to her store and tried it anyway and was amazed that it actually worked. Her customer needed very little concession and was so happy with the resolution that she placed another order. Until the manager had learned how to soothe an angry person she didn't realize that she was escalating battles for herself and that resolution was much easier when she joined the customer in solving the problem.

> When [the customer] left the building she was thanking me. So, I wanted to thank you. The piece about getting into the customer shoes and relaxing has made a big difference.
> ~Karen Kroening, Storehouse

Picture two kings in two castles. One raises the drawbridge, calls the archers to the wall and prepares the cauldrons of boiling oil. The other lowers the drawbridge and crosses the moat to greet the visitor. The first king might save his castle from an invading army, but the second king might soothe a smaller problem, preventing the army invasion altogether. We weren't dealing with invading armies.

2. Picture a fence with the problem on one side and you standing with the customer on the other side.
In working with customers we never let the fence come between the customer and us. Solving customer issues is always easier if the customer can see that we are on the same side of the fence.

> I will always remember a customer in Vermont. There was a glitch in the delivery, and I remember really wanting to understand, and told the customer I could hear in her voice how upset she was. I asked her if she could tell me what had happened that had caused such deep distress. What she told me took me by surprise. She explained that her daughter had died recently, and that her granddaughter was coming to Vermont to spend the summer with her. She wanted everything in her granddaughter's bedroom to be perfect. In an instant, everything changed; the anger was gone, and we were both talking from the heart. I am so grateful I knew how to ask the right question at the right time! ~Patty Gump, This End Up

This skill also applies in other professions. One of our colleagues completed her graduate degree in family counseling and uses the skills learned with customers.

> Last night I drew a picture of a fence with the problem on one side and the family on the other trying to solve it together. Invaluable. ~Nicole Hopkins, Storehouse

3. Presume that your company empowers you to find a way to solve problems at the first point of contact.
We encouraged people to gather all the information, research the situation, get the appropriate partner, determine at least one acceptable outcome, and call the customer with options.

When our sales associates handled customer issues, Storehouse won the customers' trust because they realized that someone was looking out for their best interests and was empowered to solve a problem. Customers respect the sales person who can make a decision and they trust the company enough to place another order. A problem becomes an opportunity.

Another advantage we found in teaching good customer service skills was that the ability to resolve customer problems transferred to good conflict-management and problem-solving. More skills ensure more successful outcomes, bolstering the courage needed to wade into problems.

As we worked on this section of the pathway, Communicate, Educate, Empower, we realized that presenting everything at once could be overwhelming and counterproductive. Despite a pressing need to work concurrently on all fronts, we learned to sharpen our focus by concentrating on one area of development at a time. Then we repeated the process. In every area of development we encouraged managers and associates to choose their own "one thing" that would make a difference in their performance. That may appear to slow the process, but we found it more effective in the long term. Choosing a meaningful "one thing" that combines challenge and attainability results in a dramatic shift in attitude, skill, and confidence.

> **We were encouraged to identify areas of personal growth (this was not seen as a weakness) and had the aid and encouragement of those around you to improve. The understanding was that the better we were, the better the business would be. ~Barb Simmons, This End Up**

A manager's role in coaching people to select an area of improvement is to help them understand that continuing to work on something they have mastered may be safe, but it doesn't move them forward. They must see that their continued success lies in their willingness to challenge themselves to the next level. ~Chris

> **I'll never forget the day when Caroline sat me down . . . to have a heart-to-heart conversation with me about my role as a struggling [district manager]. Boy, was I taking my lumps. . . . I remember she asked me what I was doing to make my district and team successful. My reply was 'I am trying to make all my managers run their stores the way I ran mine because I knew what I did was successful when I was a store manager.' She proceeded with 'Everyone wants to go from point A to B, but it's how we get there that matters.' She followed it up with 'If you want to be successful in your role, John, you must find out each manager's individual strengths and use them to make their stores successful.' Once I changed my thought process I started to see results. ~John Paladino, This End Up**

It is the individually crafted coaching approach, considering the associate's aspirations and the company goals, that inspires growth and performance improvement. You make a difference in someone's professional life and performance by helping them to isolate things to work on and to help them find success with their "one thing" and then in turn they pass along the lessons. ~Caroline

I wish I could say that the transformation to living our values was easy and immediate, but in truth, it was neither. Caroline's double dream of Storehouse making good design accessible and becoming a leadership incubator took shape slowly. Using our wheel and our ongoing development plan we observed that our managers began to change the way they interacted with their departments. People within the departments began to respond to the inclusion. When we felt discouraged, we could turn to Jim Collins's words in *Good to Great*: "No matter how dramatic the end result, the good-to-great transformations never happened in one fell swoop. There was no single defining action, no grand program, no one killer innovation, no solitary lucky break, no miracle moment. Rather, the process resembled relentlessly pushing a giant heavy flywheel in one direction, turn upon turn, building momentum until a point of breakthrough, and beyond." We became very familiar with pushing the flywheel.

Topical programs give concepts and ideals, but rarely change behavior.
We were after behavior change. ~*Caroline*

Communicate, Educate, Empower

How do you develop the relationships within the organization to ensure that the culture is connected to the customer?

Prepare your organization for change

- ✓ Educate your organization on the transitions caused by change.
- ✓ Initiate a popular tangible change to prepare people for an intangible change.
- ✓ Progress from reactive through adaptive to proactive change.

Shape your communication structure

- ✓ Establish the expectation of communication in your organization.
- ✓ Determine the methods of communication.
- ✓ Include principles of effective communication—listening, acting on feedback, and consistently giving the good and not-so-good news.

Manage by values and success principles

- ✓ Live and teach your company's values so that values will manage for you when you are not there.
- ✓ Help the managers identify what it looks like to live the values.

Understand yourself and others

- ✓ Create a leadership incubator in your organization.
- ✓ Teach change, communication, conflict, and leadership skills when times are good so they will provide a common method and vocabulary when needed.

Connect the culture to the customer

- ✓ Position the customer as the most important part of your business.
- ✓ Build customer relations skills through consistent and positive coaching of the people who interact with the customer.

Overcoming obstacles is the challenge

You may be...

✓ Identifying the causes of setbacks

✓ Facing difficulties without making them worse

✓ Maintaining a positive and proactive perspective

And the question is:
How do you handle the roadblocks?

CHAPTER 6
How Do You Handle the Roadblocks?

*Analysis will show you where your opportunities for innovation
are. Look for gaps between expected outcomes and results and
develop new ways to achieve your desired results. These opportunities are often disguised as crises. ~Caroline*

With the constant pressure for profit we admit that we did not always welcome
the roadblocks that naturally appear in every business. We learned to view them
as opportunities only as we found solutions that propelled us forward at a faster
clip. Those solutions were embedded in the skills of change management,
communication, conflict resolution, and leadership described in the previous
chapter, laying the foundation to address our roadblocks. Our issues could be
identified as business or people problems, and the two were often intertwined.

Apply Relationship Skills in
Performance Counseling

*In the Culture of Caring even the most difficult employee conversations
create opportunities for a win-win solution for both the company and
the employee. ~Caroline*

Coaching in the Culture of Caring becomes the center of improvement in every
area—selling skills, customer relations, analyzing hiring selections, creating a
merchandise grouping, planning a marketing strategy, or any other support
function. While Storehouse managers gained confidence in coaching

developmental skills and customer service issues, we also prepared them to resolve the performance issues within their departments. Although frequency is diminished, addressing poor performance is as necessary in this culture as in any other work environment. The difference is that in the Culture of Caring the most difficult situations still deserve a positive approach. Our managers found that this required more emotional quotient and more skill to navigate, but the results justified the effort. Demonstrating how to correct without damage gained the trust of everyone on the team.

The first hurdle of positive course correction was the conversation confronting the problem. Universally people share an aversion to tough conversations. A manager who enjoys tough conversations probably conducts a one-sided *"What you resist persists."*

An old saying.

diatribe, one that couldn't be labeled accurately as a discussion. These conversations can be uncomfortable for both parties, but if individuals are to grow and companies are to prosper, they can't be avoided. Left unaddressed the situation can advance from a development issue to a discipline or even a termination issue. We incorporated our managers' knowledge of individual communication, conflict management, and leadership styles to guide the conversation, taking advantage of using the same skills in multiple situations.

The longer you put off the difficult conversation the bigger it grows. Problems are not like wine; they do not improve with age. ~Caroline

When I first heard one of the values was Honest Communication, I remembered thinking well I am honest, but never realized how I would apply that in my career. Confrontation was not my favorite part of managing people, even though I valued it. I also observed others felt the same way. I do not remember the day, but I do remember [that] by not saying what needed to be said, I was not being honest. Thereafter, I found confrontation, to be a positive thing. Also when I observed someone having trouble with confrontation, I explained to them I learned in my career that telling someone something that will help them be better in their job was not confrontation, but it was really honest communication and a positive thing to do for everyone.

I continue to use these values in my career. In order to keep my focus in the right place, I found myself referring to these values. I found myself living by these values and teaching their value to others when it got down to what was really important. ~Jayne Boyd, This End Up

As in all the skills we taught, leading difficult conversations was a development process, not a training session. No manager learned to do this smoothly after one workshop. I learned to coach by observing people who did it well, and added their techniques to my own life experiences. I kept in mind what outcome was best for the company, and fortunately this outcome was usually the best for both parties as well. I started with the facts, then looked at how the other person could be viewing the situation, knowing that during the conversation my black and white data would most likely blur into shades of gray. To understand that blur I incorporated asking questions, listening, being objective, offering effective counsel, and maintaining discretion.

> *For me, leading difficult conversations requires combining my intuition and instinct with a plan. My plan envisions the ideal outcome and includes the questions that will evoke participation from my dialogue partner. While the plan is important, my intuition and instinct allow the conversation to influence my perceptions. As I drive for the next steps, I remain flexible to respond and react to the information and opinions from the other person. My questions may change, the direction may change, the ideal outcome may change. After the session I apply a post-mortem and review the outcome. The lesson comes from the difference between what I thought would happen and what actually happened. The analysis of the difference is the skill development catalyst so that I then understand the lesson for consideration for the next time. ~Caroline*

In teaching the following key elements of handling performance problems, we focused on creating a positive outcome through purposeful actions.

1. Gather facts and analyze the implications

> *When you hear no negative feedback, you may be in trouble. ~Chris*

A problem could manifest itself as friction within the team, projects not getting done, late arrivals and/or early departures, slow downs, or just tension. Usually by the time the manager recognized the problem, the team was well aware of it too.

Managers looked at the facts to determine the seriousness of the situation, to what extent it impacted business, and how it affected other members of the team.

> *When you hire good people other good people will want to join you. If you want to build a team of winners you must take action with those who aren't. The rest of your team will be watching how you handle underperforming people, so you must follow the expectations you set. Winners want to be surrounded by winners. ~Caroline*

2. Develop a plan

A comprehensive plan considers the best possible outcome for the organization and the individual, and how to make the same solution work for both. To find resolution managers needed to consider not only the facts and the impact to the company, but also how the other person could be viewing the situation. Storehouse managers had become accustomed to considering the customer's point of view when finding the best service solution and they could see the advantage of this idea in considering how their associates might view the problem they were facing. We found that this consideration helped the manager seek to understand and changed the tone of the conversation. In the planning stage a problem could appear to be a discipline or termination issue, and during the conversation the manager could realize the solution was developmental. And the reverse could be true. In the planning stage a problem could appear to be developmental and become a discipline or termination issue as new information surfaced. While it is important to start with a plan, it is equally important to be willing to change the plan.

> *"First you work on your own attitude. If your attitude is right, the things you do and say will be right."*
>
> *Sam Iorio, trainer for Dale Carnegie courses*

> *The Culture of Caring is not easy. Caring enough to help individuals grow by initiating difficult conversations is based on mutual respect and trust. It is more profitable to care because caring has a currency that is very rare. However, caring requires courage, emotional energy, and skill. ~Caroline*

3. Discussion

> *You may be imagining the best possible outcome, but use questions rather than accusations as your method of getting there. I knew that I could guide the questions, and if I watched for the opening to the solution, it would come. ~Caroline*

The respect and dignity with which difficult conversations are handled is one of the most compelling aspects of the Culture of Caring. In open and honest conversation employees can come away knowing that their managers have genuine interest in their growth and development. Focusing on facts kept the focus away from personality and accusations. It was in the discussion that the manager's skill in "ask, don't tell" played a critical role.

Included in this ask, don't tell skill was the ability to listen and allow the whole story to unfold. Sometimes in unfolding the story we faced the challenge of altering the preconceived plan because new facts were discovered. At times the situation was so altered that managers needed to take a break to consider a new best solution. Managers knew that it was wiser to make a fair decision than to make a quick one.

> *The leader's role in difficult conversations is not to dominate, but to create the environment so that you arrive together at a new action. This can take more skill, but is more likely to have a positive outcome. When you "get to where the other person is," you move toward a solution from there. The solutions stick when people come to the action plan themselves. ~Caroline*

4. Action plan for new direction with timeframes and measures

> *Everyone makes mistakes. Because we operate in a learning environment we treat mistakes as growth opportunities or teachable moments. Developing tolerance for the inevitable mistakes and developing a process to handle them allows managers to focus on coaching their teams to the next level of performance. We strive to be better tomorrow than we are today. ~Chris*

Storehouse managers resolved performance issues by initiating action plans that would position the individual to meet expectations and time frames. Assuming that we had not delayed in addressing the problem, the purpose of the action plan was to meet expectations with the necessary skill. One way of assuring that people understood the expectations was to have them write the action plan. The managers made clear what support they would offer. This could be additional training, extra coaching sessions, or setting up peer mentoring.

> **You were given the chance to prove yourself and if you fell down, then your manager was right there to pick you up and help you to figure out why you fell and to give the blessing and skills to try again. ~Angela Trevvett, This End Up and Storehouse**

5. Follow up

> *Through this method you know that if they stay they will be able to deliver the performance that meets the company's need. ~Caroline*

Along with timeframes and measures, the managers set regular follow-up conversations. These conversations started with the same fact-finding preparations. What had been the results and how did the results compare to the expectations? Keeping personalities at bay, decisions were made on acceptable progress. The follow-up meeting was not designed to force a person out of the company, but to ensure that the entire job responsibilities were covered with the greatest skill. The Culture of Caring is about results, not about relaxing standards. We now had a more concrete measurement to show whether this person was in the right job. If the person was not meeting expectations, the consequence could be termination. Although we asked for feedback and offered support, the bottom line was that we needed the right people on our team.

> **Of course there were times when all the efforts did not work and you had to let someone go, where it was just not a good fit. . . . I remember Anita, while coaching me on how to handle the dismissal . . . pointed out the impact letting someone go had on them. The many areas of their life and emotional well being that it affected. I had never thought of it in that way before. I was only thinking of how it affected me. ~Angela Trevvett, This End Up and Storehouse**

Our experience proved that developing employee relationships prevented lawsuits and government agency filings against the company. I worked for another organization that responded to government agency filings with such expertise that they won their cases. However, I observed that most of the complaints could have been avoided altogether if the communication had been better. And that was my personal mission—to impact the communication, thereby reducing the number of complaints. At This End Up and Storehouse when our managers were consistent in addressing issues through the Culture of Caring, associates tended to trust that people were treated fairly and that if a problem arose, they too would be treated fairly. People do pay attention.

After introducing our performance counseling program one important change we observed immediately was that managers were calling Chris so that she could coach them through the process before the conversation, rather than later needing help to repair an explosion.

> *Our managers had become comfortable with role-playing as a part of our selling program so we easily adapted a form of role-play to prepare them to conduct a difficult conversation. During these coaching sessions it was not uncommon to work the manager through a range of emotions as they analyzed a situation and prepared a plan. My goal was to develop their problem-solving skills and reduce the amount of time they spent in "reaction mode." I knew we were getting somewhere when a manager would call to talk about their plan rather than to vent. ~Chris*

Why did we not assign the human resources department to handle corrections? If done well, the manager-associate conversation strengthens the relationship in a way the intervention of human resources cannot accomplish. And this statement comes from me, a human resources professional. Is there a role for human resources? Absolutely. In the coaching and counseling of the manager, and sometimes the associate as well. At times, sitting in on the conversation was necessary, but the outcome was more positive for the long term if the manager led the conversation. These precepts grew at This End Up when associates or managers brought problems to my attention. I coached both the associate and the manager individually, helping them to see the situation from the other person's point of view; then they worked out their issue together. They were never going to work together productively until they had gone through this process themselves.

The executive role was to give support to the managers so that the correction was successful. There were times when we did step in to help after consulting with the manager:

✓ When we actually observed an action that needed coaching

> In one meeting, displaying my frustration about the topic, I was demonstrating an aggressive and commanding communication style. Instead of dismissing me or reprimanding me for my aggressive behavior, Chris Matthies, VP of Stores, changed topics, pulled me aside and asked if we [could] set up a time to speak. When we did meet we had a conversation that centered around my growth . . . and she helped me to understand that I too must reach out for my own professional growth. . . . That was the first time I realized I must forge my own career development with personal and professional growth. I was the typical manager just trying to do a good job. I was not clear on what becoming a leader meant. The conversation was respectful, caring, logical, and firm. I was so appreciative that she took time out of her busy day to take me to lunch and commit to me that she would commit to my professional development . . . yet I owned it. ~Christy Carpenter, Storehouse

✓ When we were asked to review a situation

One afternoon at This End Up Caroline, who was head of stores at the time, and I met with a very disgruntled former employee. We were able to dissolve her animosity and restore her dignity. The danger was over and the former employee was confident that she would find another job that was more to her liking.

How did we do that? We had a plan. We considered her point of view and imagined the most positive outcome for her. We led by asking questions, focused on her thoughts, and we listened. As she responded we revised our questions so that we were with her as she developed her own path to what she wanted for her career. The key was that she arrived at her new direction. When she knew that she was being heard, her anger dissipated. We did not offer her the job back; in fact we did not need to offer anything. She just wanted someone to hear her point of view.

> *In a nutshell you are*
>
> ✓ *Working on your own attitude*
>
> ✓ *Envisioning the outcome*
>
> ✓ *Daring to approach the issue*
>
> ✓ *Asking questions leading to the opportunity to uncover the solution.*
>
> *~Caroline*

Our difficult conversations were oral and face-to-face if possible. Using the telephone in a serious situation doesn't allow the visual body language that can contradict the responding words. And email is a bomb waiting to explode.

> *Don't use email for coaching and counseling your team. Managers show their commitment to your growth when they care enough to schedule a time to talk with you. Email might be quick but it is not an effective tool for managing people. It plays a supporting, not a primary role. ~Chris*

I have been asked how a manager should deal with the range of emotions that often accompanies difficult conversations. No one answer fits all. For instance, I have worked with people who were embarrassed at their own emotions, but wanted to continue, so we just ignored the emotion and got on with the conversation. We didn't dwell on the elephant in the room. For others a break could help. When I didn't know which approach to take, I asked. The important ingredient is respect. I learned to allow the emotion, not to be put off by it, and to have plenty of tissues handy. The emotion could also be anger. Usually anger subsides with the uninterrupted telling of the story.

The difference between the Culture of Caring and other environments is most pronounced when performance issues arise. The need for course correction required us to take action, but we learned that when we followed our process, considering the best interest of both the employee and the company, many times we were able to develop, rather than discipline.

> **The . . . 'culture' impacted my entire life. I learned how to communicate with people effectively. I learned all the aspects of the selling process that I continue to use every day. I learned how to manage with respect and care**

for your employees. I learned to continue to push and challenge those I managed with coaching and praising that was non-threatening. . . . I learned that no matter how much I thought I knew and how great I was at something I always could learn more and be better. I learned the value of listening to others and to respond honestly with open, timely communication, even the tough stuff. I learned that a manager could be a partner instead of someone to fear and criticize you. I also learned that focus, determination, drive, and support from your management could help you win. I learned the meaning of an 'open door policy.' It was a place that you could talk openly and honestly with the president and all the officers without fear of being judged or having a hidden agenda and be assured that they took your comments with a serious attitude and respect. ~Angela Trevvett, This End Up and Storehouse

So many of our lessons came from our mentor, Stewart Brown, who combined a basic love of people with a drive for profit. His human and all too real management style left room for the associate to grow and work through problems. By empowering us he made us feel successful and good about ourselves. ~Caroline

Teach Problem Solving and Root Cause Analysis

The root cause analysis is an active process in the Culture of Caring, the beginning of the solution. By solving the problem at the root using the Root Cause Analysis Method you will be able to work on the real issues. Because you are seeking the underlying cause and solving for it, you will create effective results. If you see the problem repeat, it may be because you have worked on only the surface issues and have not cured the underlying cause. ~Caroline

There is no "it's not my job" in this culture. Every business problem impacts the entire corporate population. I learned this concept years ago from my first manager at This End Up, Ashton Williams Harrison. She was a master problem solver, and we could bring her our issues; however, we were also expected to present more than one possible solution. Maybe she didn't really need my input, but she taught me to look for alternatives and that problems belonged to everyone.

At Storehouse we used two basic principles in both business and people problems as we searched for solutions:

- ✓ We needed to have the people most impacted as a part of the solution. For business problems we compiled cross-departmental teams. For people problems the people involved worked on the solution.

- ✓ We needed to find the root cause beneath the surface issues if we expected a long-term solution. This applied to both business and people problems.

Once we acknowledged the surface symptoms and analyzed the situation to uncover the real problem, we found that chaos can be a catalyst for innovation.

Solving Business Issues

When you keep focusing on what you are trying to achieve, the cycle of inclusion infuses the everyday action with the wheel and the pathway. Ask yourself if the action is in line with the pathway. Course correction is getting it back in line. ~Caroline

As we began to analyze our roadblocks to profit, Caroline set up a cross-departmental meeting structure to encourage collaboration in identifying solutions to problems that affected more than one department. These meetings brought together all the stakeholders in one room to work on shared projects or problems. The company had never had this kind of interaction and she referred to them as "Tinkertoy Meetings." We remembered playing with Tinkertoy Construction Sets, a collection of dowels that are inserted into hubs to create shapes. The Tinkertoy meetings were designed to define the problem, from the surface to the deeper issue. Participants were expected to own how their departments contributed to the problem and how they could contribute to the solution. These meetings worked only when the participants trusted each other to be searching for solutions, not blame. The result was that collaboration allowed departments to showcase their strengths and decreased the impact of their weaknesses.

For example, the Marketing Tinkertoy included representatives from merchandising, sales, finance, as well as marketing—all the stakeholders. We faced declining results from the advertising dollars spent in newspaper ads and supplements. Relying on how marketing had historically impacted sales, the group came expecting to discuss discounts, ad placement, and best circulation opportunities. Although this seemed to be the problem and the solution, by digging deeper the group acknowledged that this was a surface problem. Pouring resources into solving the surface problem would not solve the real issue. By isolating the real problem—we were not attracting our target customers—they could then determine how to direct future marketing activities. Our customer had choices other than Storehouse and we were not grabbing their attention through our Sunday supplement deals. This Tinkertoy collaboration changed the perception of the Storehouse brand by developing a multifaceted marketing approach, including research, color photography in shelter magazines, a color catalog, direct mail, and in-store events. Storehouse once again became a player in the home fashion world, influencing style, not just advertising the best bargain for the weekend.

> I was amazed at how foreign this Tinkertoy concept was to the managers. However, as they began to understand the process they could see the effectiveness of participating in the solution. Because they owned those meetings, they began to own the solutions. ~Caroline

To illustrate how Tinkertoy meetings were influencing the culture, about a year after Caroline had initiated these meetings, I facilitated a session with her executive team and prior to the workshop I casually emptied two boxes of Tinkertoys on the conference table. With no comment or instruction on the toys, we proceeded with the session. At a break I noticed that several structures had been built. The amazing thing was that they were all related. Someone had started a theme and others had contributed, which was a symbol of what we were beginning to observe in their working styles.

A second example of collaboration was the meeting we described where the store managers worked together on the sales training program. At that meeting the group uncovered a deeper problem—many customers were not being welcomed into our stores. When we began to work on the real problem, we began achieving our goal -increased sales in the friendly neighborhood store. We kept our focus on the root cause by regular mystery shops, giving us the real picture of our progress.

When we discovered the three theft rings operating at Storehouse we knew that increasing security was the answer only to the surface problem. The root cause was that employees did not feel ownership in the company. The real issue to solve was how to instill psychological ownership.

Storehouse had several stores devoted to clearance product, but we were not making clearance sales work for us. The fact that we did not have enough revenue from these stores was the obvious roadblock. Behind that roadblock we found margin issues, inventory tracking issues, and miniscule revenue from renting clearance products. Solving the deeper problems allowed us to create more revenue.

In these examples we used a problem solving technique we call the Root Cause Analysis Method. The key to arriving at the root cause is asking "and this is caused by. . . ." until the real problem is uncovered. When we could go no further we asked ourselves, "If we solve the root problem, do we also solve the surface problem?" By practicing inclusiveness and giving managers and associates a venue for discussion and debate, they rewarded us with solutions to the real problems and volunteers to enact the solutions.

Solving Relationship Issues

Growth and confidence come from meeting ever-growing challenges successfully. We believe that managers are able to meet challenges by developing skills using the Root Cause Analysis Method. Discovering the root cause is a fundamental building block of empowerment. Too often we discovered that the root cause involved people feeling bad about themselves or some action. ~Caroline

We find changing behavior to be difficult, so we applied an approach that we already understood and practiced. The Root Cause Analysis Method works for business and people problems because often the root of a business problem is a people problem. Digging to the root of the problem assured us that we were working on the real issue. Coaching for results and course correction became an integral part of Storehouse's continuing growth. Successful coaching depended on the skill of managers to determine the root cause of an employee problem and find solutions.

The Root Cause Analysis Method is one of the most powerful management development exercises I have ever witnessed. We developed this tool at This End Up, working with our district managers. As with so many of our tools, the origin of this method was Stewart Brown. One of Stewart's gifts was his ability to get to the root cause of an issue. He did it by instinct, but we had to develop a method for getting there so that we could teach the process. We watched his energy focus on what was important, avoiding distractions, questioning until he uncovered the real issue. We knew we could teach the process if our managers understood themselves and their teams, and were fostering a trusting environment.

The sessions were so successful at This End Up, that at Storehouse Chris and I extended the program to include store managers and we ended every district workshop with this management exercise.

Our managers were familiar with the root cause method of problem solving, but they had not applied the method to individual employee performance problems. Because solving people issues involved examining our own actions and reactions, we could not introduce the Root Cause Analysis Method with performance problems until we had created a trusting environment.

Creating a trusting environment takes time, but we have found that experiencing successful results causes people to open up and share their thoughts and concerns on a path to performance improvement. ~Caroline

I learned in my human resources years that in keeping records for employment issues and responding to claims of possible company misconduct, we needed to have the actual facts of a case well documented. He said, she said; he did, she did. But while that recordkeeping kept us out of trouble with state and federal regulations, by itself it did not always resolve the issues. In these management-training sessions we wanted to teach managers to resolve the issues.

In the first round of our root cause sessions, the managers brought a difficult management situation, confident that we would fix that associate who was causing so much discord. Imagine their surprise when we did not work on that associate; we focused on the manager's interaction with the person. We maintain that we can only work on ourselves, but by working on our own action and reaction we can change another person's reaction. Our approach to improving the situation presented by these managers used the strengths of communication, conflict, and leadership styles that we had already identified.

We found that the managers in the group identified not only with the issue that they had presented, but often they were wrestling with a situation similar to one that another manager presented. This enabled them to go back to their teams with new approaches for multiple situations. This was not about discipline; it was about development.

> When you open yourself to this kind of dialogue, you may hear anything. People will be watching your body language and expression in addition to listening to your response. Until you have the composure to hear the good and bad, you ought to refrain from this exercise. Develop your confidence in your ability to ask the best questions to work toward a constructive solution. ~Caroline

Every situation brought to our sessions was not about individual and corporate course correction. We also worked with positive situations involving talented associates whom the managers sought to help in maximizing their growth.

Because we were sharing performance experiences we were ever mindful of the need for discretion. The depth of the impression of discretion is critical in a trusting environment.

The follow-through to results was challenging. The store managers left the sessions with a plan for working with an associate, but it took courage to address the issue back at the store. The district manager left the sessions with 10-12 different plans to coach. The good news is that each time we used this method it became smoother. The managers became more accustomed to digging beneath the surface to find the real issue. The district managers became more skillful coaches, and we all became better listeners. At stake was the success of our team, and therefore our business.

Perhaps the most rewarding part of leading a company is witnessing the managers as they grow in understanding themselves and others. ~Caroline

We found that hurdling roadblocks using our principles became easier with practice. The Tinkertoy meetings became cooperative venues for participants to accomplish projects together. The Root Cause Analysis Method, uncovering real issues, became powerful avenues for business and performance development. The managers began to trust enough to coach one another and they welcomed every breakthrough they experienced. Teaching skills to work with customers paved the way for teaching skills on internal relationships. I remember an "Aha" moment with our managers when one of them stopped mid-sentence and said, "I get it. We are using the same principles with the people we manage as we do with our customers." I suddenly saw a flywheel spinning. The Culture of Caring at work.

Coach for Results & Course Correction

How do you use relationship skills to find the solution? How do you practice the Root Cause Analysis Method to determine the right problem to solve in both business and people issues?

Apply relationship skills in performance counseling

- ✓ Address performance issues in a timely manner and give your feedback in a way that is constructive and developmental.

- ✓ View issues from the other person's perspective before making a decision.

- ✓ Set expectations high enough so that standards are met when expectations are met.

- ✓ Be willing to take action if expectations are not met.

Teach problem solving and root cause analysis

- ✓ Find the root cause of a problem and determine if you will cure the surface issues by curing the source of the problem.

- ✓ Use collaboration between individuals and departments to solve problems and foster ownership

- ✓ Teach people to think and they will solve problems.

PATHWAY TO PROFIT
PART 3

Creating a Continuing Cycle of Improvement

"Very few things in this world are cast-iron;
most things are papier-mâché."

Peter Drucker

Maintaining the momentum
is the challenge

You may be...

✓ Facing competitive changes

✓ Discovering new opportunities

✓ Taking advantage of advanced technology and processes

And the question is:
What's next?

CHAPTER 7
What's Next?

Just when you are congratulating yourself on your successful culture shift, you will find a new gap and realize the fun starts again. Dust off your Pathway to Profit. ~Caroline

We've traveled the Pathway to Profit, and at the end of our pathway we have placed a circle depicting the Process of Continual Improvement. As the circle implies, this is a never-ending process. The work doesn't end when the culture shifts. The difference is that the team works at a more advanced pace in an environment of willing cooperation. Culture is the core of the company's ongoing continual improvement—taking action . . . evaluating results . . . creating a new plan . . . taking action. . . .

The Process of Continual Improvement

This continual improvement is process management, not project management. However, if project management is your forte, you can break the process into tasks that are linked together with an eye toward achieving the desired improvement. ~Caroline

As we saw the culture take shape at Storehouse we began to welcome our change opportunities because we were working with people who had learned to embrace change. We were ever evolving. The problem solved yesterday gave us a new challenge to identify today and opened a new opportunity for tomorrow.

Marketing

As we shifted our marketing focus from newspaper inserts to a broader out-reach, we faced the challenge of making good design accessible in venues beyond our stores. We started with a small color catalog and grew the catalog business, dovetailing it with interactive online access. A major consideration in that decision was how to make all venues mutually supportive. Our stores allowed customers to see and touch products that they viewed in catalogs and online. Catalog and online shopping created convenience for customers who were not able to visit the store. It didn't end there. Creating interest outside our store range opened increased marketing possibilities. Our furniture began to appear in feature articles in shelter magazines. Oprah's Angel Network Katrina Homes Registry, the homes she built for Hurricane Katrina evacuees were furnished with Storehouse furniture. We supported ABC's *Extreme Home Makeover* with furniture for one of their homes. *Queer Eye for the Straight Guy,* a popular HGTV series, used Storehouse furniture. Our continual improvement took us far beyond the Sunday supplement.

Education

Increased exposure in the home fashion world changed the Storehouse brand. Many customers visiting our stores had seen us on television, in magazines, or online, and were expecting their homes to be transformed by our products. Meanwhile back at the store, we had been concentrating on our selling skills and developing customer relationships, contributing to the Storehouse brand change. Customers began to trust that we were really interested in them, so they shared their ideas. Our fashion reputation, combined with our customer approach, led to an opportunity to satisfy the customer need for design service. We had trained designers throughout the company, but our goal was to have every associate learn to be a design consultant. Storehouse's continual improvement was mid-range price points and complimentary design service in a friendly neighborhood store. Viewing customer needs as lifestyle changes, rather than selling a sofa, increased revenue at Storehouse and satisfaction for the customer.

We started our educational workshops with the sales team because our most pressing need was to increase revenue to improve our profit picture. Although the other departments understood the urgency, it wasn't long before managers in distribution and the home office asked me to create a development program for their teams.

Logistics

Reorganizing a distribution center to handle much larger volumes was just a start on the advances we were able to make in more efficient service. Our continued sales growth meant that volume increased, challenging the warehouse crew to work in the same amount of space. As they handled ever-increasing product deliveries, the old method of visual sighting to identify items was growing more difficult. It was taking too long to load a truck. We needed a more precise storage method. Scott Downs led our information technology department as they worked with distribution to install an inventory barcode system informing stockers where to store merchandise. Pullers were then able to use the barcode to locate the merchandise for delivery. Continual improvement.

And how would we describe the people of Storehouse as our pathway unfolded? Introspection and self-analysis became a way of life, with individual growth a byproduct of our communication and development program. They supported one another in their quest to be better today than yesterday. Teams worked together for solutions instead of casting blame. There were no theft rings because the associates "owned" the company. They remained loyal through adversity and most will tell you that Storehouse was the best place they ever worked.

> **Caroline, I was thinking about things to be thankful for, and in my professional life, I am most thankful for you finding yourself at the helm of this wacky ship called Storehouse, and assembling such a wonderful team. ~Kim Britt, Storehouse**

The Storehouse culture shift was dramatic and brought recognition from our industry.

Michelle Lamb, a national and international speaker on trends in the furniture industry, commented to us that she had never seen anything like the camaraderie and genuine authenticity of the good feelings and relationships at Storehouse.

Recognition came from the WithIt organization (Women In the Home Furnishings Industry) in awarding our president the education award. We won the ART Association's award for two consecutive years. Home Magazine named Storehouse the Home Furnishings Retailer of the Year. The next year we were named the Catalog Success Entrepreneur of the Year.

More important, however, is the recognition our customers gave us. They voted with their wallets and rewarded our efforts with effervescent sales.

We realized the vision of being the friendly neighborhood store, making good design readily accessible through our merchandise selections and our knowledgeable sales force. We served our customers through our stores, by telephone, and by Internet. We delivered our products with efficiency and care, and we supported our sales and delivery teams with more efficient back office systems. An amazing comeback for the struggling company Caroline joined.

> *In the end it's all about authenticity, truly caring about your customers, your co-workers, your vendors, and the profitability of your company. ~Dixon*

Our quest wasn't easy, but it was worthwhile for the people who worked with us and for the profit we realized through our process of continual improvement.

We know the value of improving the world, one associate, one relationship at a time.

These are just a few comments about what it meant to work in the Culture of Caring at Storehouse.

> **Thanks for teaching me how to be a better person. ~Brien Cooley, Storehouse**

> **I will never forget you and the inspirations you have passed on to me. ~Sharon Schmitz, Storehouse**

> **Chris, I don't know what to say but thank you. Thank you for believing in me and your commitment to my success. ~Tom Holmwood, Storehouse**

> **I want to thank you from the bottom of my heart for all you have done for the company and for my development as a store manager and as a person. These were all life lessons we were learning, not just workplace lessons. ~Dan Bauder, Storehouse**

What our colleagues have just described tells about the cultural environment, but what about profit? We doubled our sales in four years, reversed a double-digit loss, set the company on an innovative path, and we developed people who used new skills to change the culture, merge two companies, and achieve profitability. We helped people feel good about themselves.

Process of Continual Improvement

*How do you maintain momentum
on the Pathway to Profit, continuing
the process of improvement?*

✓ Search for ways to improve the accessibility of products and service to customers.

✓ Study current industry practices, looking for innovative opportunities.

✓ Evolve educational programs to meet the organization's growth and change opportunities.

✓ Update recognition programs to reward targeted goal achievement.

✓ Challenge your organization to expand the boundaries of possibility.

AFTERWORD

"Everything will be all right in the end;
and if it's not all right, it's not the end."

Movie, *The Best Exotic Marigold Hotel*

AFTERWORD

Strength and resiliency are built through the combination of success and adversity, and we have experienced both. As we researched the next step in sharing the Culture of Caring, we observed the business world's interest in the impact of culture. What prompted us to write is the realization that no one who has actually developed the culture in an organization has ever explained exactly how they did it. This book is our attempt to tell you how we did it. ~Caroline

Our story would not be complete without sharing what happened to these two very special companies that spawned the Culture of Caring.

With such a strong culture, such outstanding financial success, and such loyal associates and customers, you may want to search for our This End Up in Richmond, Virginia. You won't find it.

And you won't find our Storehouse in Atlanta, Georgia.

Both companies achieved financial success through the culture and both ended as the result of technological changes gone awry.

At This End Up, almost ten years after Stewart and Libby's departure, our president committed the company to outsourcing our delivery service to a third party whose computer system did not interface with ours, nor did their company values. "It's not my job" was their attitude when our store computer system could not link with their warehouse system, preventing us from retrieving the correct product to fill customer orders. The price tag to fix the resulting customer issues was enormous, causing us to bleed cash so quickly we could not save this company that a year earlier had been a healthy, profitable business with its best sales year ever. This End Up was liquidated twenty-six years after the party that started it all.

Like in life, when havoc abounds the strong grow stronger. The impact that [This End Up's] culture had on me grew when all hell broke loose.

We as a company were close to losing everything we stood for and everything that we worked hard to make happen. Everything we were proud of was close to breaking. We began dealing with a partner company that didn't embrace the Shared Values.

The tone of [This End Up] began to shift with people from the partner company. . . . Yet, even as the tone of the company shift was taking hold, I saw the strength of a larger group of people that embraced the . . . culture and ached to hold on to it. I joined THAT group and became a part of the tug of war in the work version of *the good, the bad, and the ugly*. In the end, both sides walked away bruised and beaten but because of the strength of the Shared Values and the want for the Culture of Caring many of us took bits and pieces of the culture with us to new adventures.

The aspect of the . . . Culture that had the most impact on my growth and development was the caring. I don't mean the holy grail of being altruistic, but just being in touch with what you do and the wave of impact that follows: Fight the fight without sticks and stones. Climb the ladder of success and take others with you.

It has made me a better professional, and more profoundly, a better person. ~Barbara Gionti, This End Up

While Storehouse maintained a sustained growth mode our sister company, Rowe Manufacturing, initiated a problem-ridden technological change in their operating system and found themselves in financial trouble. Within eight months they lost millions in manufacturing revenue when they were unable to fulfill orders in a timely fashion. Storehouse had to continue to rely upon Rowe as our principal upholstery supplier, and thus we too suffered the lead-time shift from four weeks to four months. For the first time we experienced a loss of sales and carefully cultivated customer good will. Our parent company filed for bankruptcy protection. Although Storehouse had not been responsible for the system problems, in order to gain the money they needed, Rowe liquidated its most available asset, Storehouse. Our inventory was sold to satisfy Rowe's bank debt and within eight weeks the company we had rescued ceased to be.

During that shocking period of our liquidation, I kept a Mother Teresa quote on my desk, "What you spend years building, someone could destroy overnight; build anyway." ~Dixon

Validation for Storehouse's untenable position came from industry experts:

A national home furnishings retail consultant from the strategy side of the industry sat across the table from Caroline at meetings during the bankruptcy crisis, just staring at her. Later he emailed her to say that in all his consulting experience "I had never seen department heads so closely aligned as at Storehouse. I kept trying to figure out how you did it, especially in a crisis."

"Caroline, I am truly amazed by the cohesiveness of your team. In my 20-plus years of doing turnarounds I have never seen a team hang as tough as yours."

Even a vice president of the company that liquidated us said that Storehouse was a company that should never have been liquidated.

A human resources professional from another company asked to talk with Caroline because she wanted to meet "the person who was head of two companies where everyone I see says the same things: 'I felt like I mattered there.' 'I felt like I grew and learned new things.' 'I had better skills, both personal and professional than when I started.' 'I felt like I could impact my environment.'"

A poignant comment from a customer:

"I am so sad about Storehouse's closing. That was a great store—from the selection of furniture and accessories to the excellent service provided by the staff. It was a great source of things that a) didn't look like everything else . . . b) were contemporary without being too 'out there' and c) were pretty reasonably priced. Aside from grief therapy, is there anything else you can suggest in terms of sources for the price, style, and selection equivalent to Storehouse?"

> **I wanted you to know that if you have had moments of doubting what you have accomplished in a short time frame as to rooting culture, and developing people to take charge, take ownership, and a higher calling to customer service excellence, you need doubt no longer. . . . I am surrounded by a team who performs small and large miracles every day and are absolutely 'getting' what you have attempted to do for them, for the business, and for the customer . . . they have these gifts to take into the future (priceless). ~Rosita Suhs, This End Up and Storehouse**

Life is always a journey. You are never there. You experience mileposts that let you know that you are making progress. It is as dynamic a process as people are. ~Caroline

In writing this book, we "face the brutal reality" as recommended by Jim Collins in his book *Good to Great*, and we know that you could be asking yourself, "Why would I want to follow a pathway bringing success to companies that ended in bankruptcy?" Why indeed? "Just because a company falls doesn't invalidate what we can learn by studying that company when it was at its historical best." Jim Collins, as quoted in the *New York Times*.

In neither company did the culture lead to bankruptcy. In fact, both companies achieved success because of the culture and wouldn't have been worthy stories at all without it. The crate furniture style of This End Up could have peaked and waned without the magic of the people who built, sold, and delivered the products, with the full support of those who worked behind the scenes. After all, a furniture line is not expected to last for twenty-six years. Without a culture shift Storehouse was on a path trending downward as other brands outpaced them in style and accessibility. With the focus on the customer, neither This End Up nor Storehouse lost its customer base, even in the most trying of times, and this loyalty was due to our commitment to the Culture of Caring and its impact on the brands we built. We are aware of the financial and operational pitfalls of running a successful business. Bankruptcy closings have taught us lessons we never wanted to learn.

After the closing of Storehouse Caroline was asked to speak at the Furniture/Today Leadership Conference.

The legacy of the company will reside in our team-members as they spread their incredible talent out to other companies. I am excited to envision our team, off in new ways, sharing our teachings and their development as they meld into their new worlds.

We have heard amazing stories from our staff since they have been in the recruited mode, and from those that are recruiting them—comments like "the best interviewee I have ever had" to "the culture and values and skills that are consistently present in Storehouse people are amazing" and "if I hire them will it translate to my company?"

One leading furniture company executive who has been watching Storehouse for a while asked a couple of interesting questions that relate to our topic. This executive and his company had been interested in the energy and warmth that emanated from the Storehouse stores. They hired researchers to look at our catalog and compare it to others and when their focus group respondents said they preferred our catalog compared to the other three leading lifestyle merchants, and the reason why was that we were warm and inviting . . . I had to smile.

Well, we did change the conversation at Storehouse, and we changed the culture, and we transformed the workplace into a place where many of our staff have now told us that this was indeed the best working experience of their lives. One example is the way the organization performed in crisis. Not one manager, senior manager, district manager, regional manager, vice president, or director left Storehouse during its difficult period. We saw so many heroes push through to the end. Why? We made Storehouse a place where people felt that they were developed personally and professionally. My belief is that when you create an environment that taps into enlightened self-interest of others, powerful forces start to work. We saw it happen here. ~Caroline

We stand with you on a bridge between where we have been and where we are going. The four of us have started new ventures, helping other businesses succeed. It has been gratifying to realize that the problems we observe within other organizations have answers somewhere along the Pathway. The Culture of Caring intertwines people and profit, building businesses and affecting the world—one person at a time.

Meeting you, Stewart Brown, and working for [This End Up] were life-changing events and influence how I live my life each and every day. . . . For the last 16 years I have worked for . . . a privately owned mattress retailer in the L.A. area. . . . A very important lesson I learned from you, Stewart, is what they needed was to develop and care about people [and that] would directly affect the bottom line. . . . With a lot of hard work and commitment we have had great success. . . . I have one day left before I retire . . . last week [my company] gave me a surprise tribute with a slide show of fond memories of our journey and lots of kind words. I was so humbled to hear how much of an impression I made on so many people. This tribute was really not all about me, Stewart, it was about you and the ripple effect of how you and the [This End Up] team inspired and touched not only my life, but all of [this] team's lives too. This End Up gave me the ability to create a pretty special job and life for myself and the gift of being able to inspire a lot of people.

I just want to thank you and to tell you that you made a huge difference in many people's lives. ~Fay McLean, This End Up

Through the evergreen principles of the Culture of Caring we influenced people who were as diverse as in any workforce. It didn't matter if they drove a truck, moved furniture in a warehouse, built furniture, worked in the office or a store, their needs to be included and appreciated were more alike than different. Technological advances in communication did not seem to diminish the craving for connection in the workplace. We appealed to the individual attention that they wanted and provided the inclusive group so that they could belong to something bigger than themselves. Whatever the background, the language, the age, or the work experience, they responded to our culture—realizing that we listened and respected their ideas, that we challenged them to exceed their expectations, that they owned their own development, and that we recognized them as important to the team.

> *If you want to make a positive difference in the world, why not begin right where you are? Start with the person next to you at work. Try providing an environment in which people can grow and develop and you can make a positive difference in the lives of the people who pass through that environment. Because we spend the majority of our time at work, we can reach so many people in this practical way. The effect radiates out to their families, friends, and others, too. ~Caroline*

ADDENDUM

"I've learned that people will forget what you said,
people will forget what you did, but people will never,
never forget how you have made them feel."

Maya Angelou

INCLUSIVE OPPORTUNITIES

Inclusiveness is a key element in the Culture of Caring. Throughout the book we have shared many opportunities to make people feel a part of any organization, and in this section we have compiled the ideas for easy reference. These opportunities are not all new projects, maybe just new methods. Including managers and associates in the building of an organization brings loyalty and commitment.

Suggestions

1. Join the group for informal gatherings—be a part of the "lunch bunch."

2. Consider an alternative to the massive "boss's" desk that has the two little chairs on the other side.

3. Before you embark on a culture change, schedule individual meetings with each person on your team to get to know the visions of the people who report directly to you.

4. Introduce participative management by holding group meetings with your team to generate the sales and profit ideas that will carry you forward.

5. Have each manager write a job description for each job in the department, and encourage the person actually doing the job to compile the basic list of responsibilities and tasks.

6. Involve other managers in the interviewing and evaluation process to reinforce the skill of analysis in all the interviewing managers and strengthen the culture and values.

7. With the end goal of collaboratively building the vision, ask all the people in every department to describe the ideal company where they would like to work.

8. Set up a cross-departmental meeting structure to offset the silo system and encourage collaboration in achieving goals that affect more than one department. "Tinkertoy Meetings."

9. Come down from the ivory tower, the ultimate silo.

10. Seek company improvement ideas from every individual and incorporate those ideas in your goal planning session. After company and department goals are determined, return to the individuals to solidify their commitment for their part to play.

11. Offer a workshop so that everyone on the team understands the creativity-meeting model and will not let anyone stampede an idea through, nor allow anyone to squelch a teammate's idea.

12. Use your creative meeting room to serve the needs of your behind-the-scenes staff. Not only is it a good utilization of space, but it also keeps the financial, technology, and other back office departments informed of the company direction, making them feel a part of that direction.

13. Host a gala event to critique new products or services, combining feedback and fun.

14. Encourage each individual to select one thing to work on at a time, a personal skill that will impact professional performance.

15. Communicate so regularly that associates don't need to worry that there may be something that they don't know. Communication alleviates the fear of the unknown.

16. Coordinated meetings, conference calls, newsletters, email, social media, and snail mail all serve to include everyone in information sharing.

17. Create occasions to recognize associates' accomplishments, both orally and in print.

18. Provide opportunities for participants to take leadership roles in meetings and communications.

19. Bring managers together to compile the actions they must take to demonstrate the culture to the employee in all the phases of an employee's career with you.

20. Include managers in each other's growth by working in small groups with people who trust each other and who are not shy about helping others to see themselves as others see them.

21. Teach leadership and communication skills in groups of peers where people trust each other because they become accustomed to different styles. The more they know about the styles, the easier it will be to coach the people they manage.

22. Gather together representatives of the people who interact with your customers and learn about their practices and ideals. Find out where they see the gap between practice and ideal.

23. Include everyone in learning how to handle the customer who has an issue. It may take specialized skill to solve the problem, but everyone should be able to reassure the customer that the problem can be solved.

24. Make your associates feel like owners by having them bring you more than one possible solution when they bring you a problem.

RECOMMENDED READING

Bossidy, Larry, Ram Charan, and Charles Burck. *Execution: the Discipline of Getting Things Done*. New York: Crown, 2002. Print.

When we worked on accountability, *Execution* verified that we were on a track other successful companies had used to achieve desired results. For example, the authors' concepts regarding setting goals, coaching, changing behavior, and rewarding for behavior as well as results, were already firmly imbedded in our Pathway to Profit principles.

Bridges, William. *Managing Transitions. Making the Most of Change*. New York: Perseus, 1991. Print.

William Bridges taught us how to manage the personal part of change. We knew that upcoming changes would affect people as well as business, and by sharing his book we were able to guide whole companies through difficult and complex transitions.

Coffman, Curt, and Gabriel Gonzalez- Molina. *Follow this Path: How the World's Greatest Organizations Drive Growth by Unleashing Human Potential*. New York: Warner Books, 2002. Print.

We were interested to see that the Gallup Organization had mapped a path to success that required getting the right person in the right place, just as we had discovered in our first company, This End Up, where we learned the foundation of the Culture of Caring.

Collins, Jim. *Good to Great: Why Some Companies Make the Leap . . . and Others Don't*. New York: HarperCollins, 2001. Print.

Good to Great is mentioned several times in our book. We discovered Jim Collins's book just as we were embarking on the difficult transition from massive deficit to profitability. Three concepts particularly applied to our situation—to confront our brutal realities, to expect to continue to push the flywheel, and to realize that our success would initially appear in small increments.

Connors, Roger, Tom Smith, and Craig Hickman. *The Oz Principle: Getting Results through Individual and Organizational Accountability*. New York: Portfolio, 2004. Print.

Finding the title, *The Oz Principle,* led us to think that we would be able to add a bit of fun in the difficult task of teaching managers and associates to assume accountability for their own success. We did make the process fun, and we began to refer to their concept of acting above or below "the line," working toward "see it, own it, solve it, do it."

The 4 Roles of Leadership. Franklin Covey, 1999. Print.

This short book was part of a seminar sponsored by the Franklin Covey organization. We found that our Pathway to Profit included concepts they described as the "Six Rights –right processes, right structure, right people, right information, right decisions, right rewards."

Freiberg, Kevin, and Jackie Freiberg. *Nuts! Southwest Airlines' Crazy Recipe for Business and Personal Success*. Austin: Bard, 1998. Print.

We were so excited about *Nuts!* that we invited both Kevin and Jackie Freiberg (in different years) to speak to our management group. We wanted our managers to know that a large, well-known company had developed a culture that included focus on individual growth and a sense of fun.

Gladwell, Malcolm. *Blink: The Power of Thinking Without Thinking*. New York: Time Warner, 2005. Print.

For our transition to profit, the single most important concept in *Blink* was that building relationships with our customers could be the deciding factor in our success.

---. *The Tipping Point: How Little Things Can Make a Big Difference*. New York: Little, Brown, 2002. Print.

The Tipping Point reinforced the idea that we needed to build the pieces—the brand, the development program, manager-associate communication and growth, and customer relationships—trusting that we would reach a "tipping point" where the culture would create the success we were seeking.

Goleman, Daniel, Richard Boyatzis, and Annie McKee. *Primal Leadership: Realizing the Power of Emotional Intelligence*. Boston: Harvard Business Press, 2002. Print.

Primal Leadership was an important addition to our leadership incubator program. The six styles of leadership the authors describe influenced our ability to see ourselves as we were seen by the people we managed. Knowing our innate styles allowed us to learn how to employ other styles in the most appropriate situations.

Kroeger, Otto, and Janet Thuesen. *Typetalk at Work: How the 16 Personality Types Determine Your Success on the Job*. New York: Dell, 1992. Print.

Knowing that managers must understand themselves before they could influence their teams, we turned to Myers-Briggs Type Indicator® as a teaching tool. *Type Talk at Work* was our choice of texts because it is a basic discussion of the different communication styles and how they impact the workplace. This was the first of a series of learning experiences aimed at understanding and accepting differences.

Mitchell, Jack. *Hug your Customers: the Proven Way to Personalize Sales and Achieve Astounding Results*. New York: Hyperion Books, 2003. Print.

". . . [A] hug is anything that exceeds a customer's expectations." Such a simple concept was a great teaching tool. Our managers and associates could immediately recall incidents when they had gone above and beyond what their customers expected and they felt good about sharing these successes. The group recognition gave them determination to repeat their actions, and try ideas that had worked for others.

Patterson, Kerry, Joseph Grenny, Ron McMillan, and Al Switzler. *Crucial Confrontations: Tools for Resolving Broken Promises, Violated Expectations, and Bad Behavior*. New York: McGraw-Hill, 2004. Print.

---. *Crucial Conversations: Tools for Talking When Stakes Are High*. New York: McGraw-Hill, 2002. Print.

A manager recommended these two books because he thought their ideas were very similar to what we were teaching; and we agreed. One of the most important concepts that the authors share is the mindset necessary for successful outcomes in difficult situations—"What do I want for me? What do I want for others? What do I want for the relationship?"

Peters, Thomas, and Robert Waterman. *In Search of Excellence: Lessons from America's Best-run Companies*. New York: Harper & Row, 1982. Print.

In Search of Excellence was a major influence in describing the culture that made This End Up so successful. The book encouraged us to identify the values that drove the culture. By writing our "Shared Values" newcomers were able to determine if they were a match for the company and were aware of what would be expected. As the business spanned the country and the culture evolved, this melding of instinct with structure bonded managers and associates in a way that our colleagues still remember.

von Oech, Roger. *A Whack on the Side of the Head: How You Can Be More Creative*. New York: Warner Books, 1998. Print.

When we concentrated on unleashing creativity within our organization, we turned to *A Whack on the Side of the Head.* Just the name promised a zany approach to looking at different possibilities. Our program was fun and the group learned a successful idea-generation model.

Yokoyama, John, and Joseph Michelli. *When Fish Fly: Lessons for Creating a Vital and Energized Workplace from the World Famous Pike Place Fish Market*. New York: Hyperion Books, 2004. Print.

We had heard of the Pike Place Fish Market, but we questioned how we could use their fish-throwing concept in our businesses. *When Fish Fly* illustrates how a company can change when the owner alters his leadership style to create an empowered culture. Surprisingly, the associates of this little fish market determined that they wanted to be world famous. Their story is the epitome of using fun and inclusiveness to capture associate and customer loyalty; and that concept was very applicable to our business.

SUGGESTED WORKSHOPS

- ✓ Selecting Associates
- ✓ Recognizing Strengths and Opportunities for Improvement
- ✓ Performance Management
- ✓ Accepting Accountability
- ✓ Unleashing Creativity
- ✓ Building Brand Through Marketing and Merchandising
- ✓ Managing Change
- ✓ Managing by Success Principles
- ✓ Understanding Communication Preferences
- ✓ Managing Conflict
- ✓ Discovering Your Leadership Style
- ✓ Coaching for Development
- ✓ Selling Skills
- ✓ Sales Coaching
- ✓ Making Good Design Accessible
- ✓ Soothing the Angry Customer
- ✓ Guiding Difficult Conversations
- ✓ Applying the Root Cause Analysis Method

Tracking Your Success

Create an organizational architecture for profitable growth

- ❑ Research: Identify your opportunities/identify your problems
- ❑ Create a working hypothesis
- ❑ Assemble/reassemble your team
- ❑ Conduct internal interviews with team
- ❑ Develop job descriptions
- ❑ Establish interviewing questions and structure around the needs of the company
- ❑ Create collaboratively your mission, vision, common set of working values
- ❑ Write 3-5 year strategic plan
- ❑ Develop annual operating plan
- ❑ Break operating plan into department goals
- ❑ Establish correlating individual goals
- ❑ Align individual goals with department goals which align with company goals
- ❑ Create performance metrics
- ❑ Analyze your strengths and weaknesses
- ❑ Establish a creativity process: art, science, analysis, trend structure

Create the culture for company relationships focused on the customer

- ❑ Hire a development guru
- ❑ Develop an education plan
- ❑ Establish your communications architecture
- ❑ Align your rewards program with your expectations

❑ Begin skill development exercises

> ❑ Crystallize Your Vision
>
> ❑ Select Associates
>
> ❑ Recognize Strengths and Opportunities for Development
>
> ❑ Accept Accountability
>
> ❑ Unleash Creativity
>
> ❑ Build Brand
>
> ❑ Manage Change
>
> ❑ Manage by Success Principles
>
> ❑ Understand Communication Preferences
>
> ❑ Manage Conflict
>
> ❑ Understand Leadership Styles
>
> ❑ Coach for Development
>
> ❑ Coach Selling Skills
>
> ❑ Soothing the Angry Customer
>
> ❑ Guide Difficult Conversations
>
> ❑ Apply the Root Cause Analysis Method

The process of continual improvement

❑ Set up the evaluation and assessing process for ongoing improvement

❑ Measure results

❑ Follow-up

ACKNOWLEDGMENTS

A Pathway to Profit is the story of thousands of people who created the essence of This End Up and Storehouse. In our narrative we mention some of the players who made the story possible: Stewart Brown, Libby Brown, Steve Robertson, Randy Ward, Sara Flemer Simpson, Christina Bienick, Ashton Williams Harrison, and Scott Downs. There are many more.

Our gratitude goes to our colleagues from both companies who sent their comments which we used to demonstrate the effect of the pathway: Rich Scarfo, Jayne Boyd, John Paladino, Margaret Breuer, Mark Ferraro, Kiom Maraschiello, Barbara Gionti, Jane Toney, Barb Simmons, Michael Young, Fabio Ruberto, Bill Levine, Blake Spicer, Debbie Robbins, Cathy Pirtle, Ann McCormack, Christy Carpenter, Mary Warner Hart, Jennifer Spencer, Sandy Kohut MacDonald, Michael Norris, Barbara Ross, Cathy Caples, Kathy Tierney, Kim Britt, Sharon Schmitz, Elizabeth McKernan, Karen Kroening, Patty Gump, Nicole Hopkins, Angela Trevvett, Brien Cooley, Tom Holmwood, Dan Bauder, Rosita Suhs and Fay McLean.

We quoted other wise business leaders throughout the book, including our friend, Karen McNeill.

Our cover and graphics were designed by Steven Davenport of CrossEye, Inc.

Thank you also to our friends who read early drafts and gave such valuable feedback that we were able to revise and edit again and again and again! Flo Graham, Martha Branch, Lit Maxwell, Joe Carroll, Libby Brown, Marilyn Shaw, Mark Aesch, and Greg Smith.

We are appreciative of the support we received from our families as we nurtured the Culture of Caring through two companies and the writing of this book.

THE AUTHORS

Anita Pugh, this book's narrator, is a human resources and leadership training consultant with HB2 Resources. She coaches managers and creates training and development programs to achieve company initiatives. Her specialty is building the culture that involves people in their own growth and the success of the organization. Anita lives in Richmond, VA.

Caroline Hipple, a principal partner and "chief energy officer" of HB2 Resources, is an industry strategist helping companies to actualize their creative visions. Passionate about the business of design and the design of business, she created the Pathway to Profit structure to be a guide as she led the team through the financial and cultural turnaround of a struggling company. Caroline lives in Atlanta, GA.

Chris Matthies is a leadership training consultant with HB2 Resources. She is highly regarded for her expertise in sales leadership and people development, both in the classroom and as leader of a department. Her specialty is establishing cultural behaviors that maximize performance. Chris lives in Virginia Beach, VA.

Dixon Bartlett, a founding partner of HB2 Resources, positions himself as the partnership's "agent provocateur." A master of merchandising design and presentation, he is well recognized for his trend-forward aesthetic. Backgrounds in product development and sales management converge as he weighs how an organization's brand affects the perception of both the public and the people within the company. Dixon lives in Atlanta, GA.

DIXON, CHRIS, ANITA, CAROLINE
BLAKE BURTON, PHOTOGRAPHER